Percy Russell

**The Literary Manual**

A Complete Guide to Authorship

Percy Russell

**The Literary Manual**
*A Complete Guide to Authorship*

ISBN/EAN: 9783337402006

Printed in Europe, USA, Canada, Australia, Japan

Cover: Foto ©Thomas Meinert / pixelio.de

More available books at **www.hansebooks.com**

# THE

# LITERARY MANUAL;

OR,

## A Complete Guide to Authorship.

BY

## PERCY RUSSELL.

London:

LONDON LITERARY SOCIETY,

376, STRAND, W.C.

———

1886.

# CONTENTS.

## Part I.

## Part II.

# *Contents.*

# THE LITERARY MANUAL;

OR,

## A COMPLETE GUIDE TO AUTHORSHIP.

𝕻𝖆𝖗𝖙 𝕴.

# I.—INITIAL.

## *Literary Technics.*

IT is now universally admitted that sound technical knowledge is indispensable to success in the recognised
arts and industries of modern life, with almost all of which
it is daily more closely associated. Our times are super-
eminently practical, and all supreme success is denied to
men or women, however gifted with Genius, and rich in
natural endowments, who can not, or do not, cultivate
the *technique* of the vocation they adopt.

This being so, it seems strange that while every other
legitimate pursuit has a special technology, Literature has
no manual of practical Literary Technics, no complete and
trustworthy guide, which would enable an inexperienced
writer, to give his work that technical form and finish,
which commands from Publishers' Readers, and Editors,
an attentive consideration, which the crude outpourings of
even genius never obtain.

I speak, of course, of the working technics of literature
whereby an amateur might become professional. There
are books on Authors, and Authorship, and ample
instruction in the rules of English composition, but no clear
account exists of the method for obtaining this transforma-
tion. Yet every professional writer first began as an ama-

teur ; the *period* of transition varies enormously, but the *method* is practically similar.

If, then, we are correct, the successful writer must acquire the technics of literature—just as the painter must have his manipulative and mechanical skill—and the success of his writings will be proportioned to the *thoroughness* of his knowledge of Literary Technology or—his original ability,—if his knowledge of the Technology be great, his advantage will be enormous ; if it be small, his genius even will be comparatively lost. Now this, like other knowledge, can be vicariously acquired by means of proper instruction. This special knowledge can, indeed, be easily acquired from a book, and it is the object of the present work to supply a Manual that shall leave no technical or business point in the Literary Life unexplained or obscure, and that shall fully equip the author for the work to be done in the most effective manner. Now, Literary Technology possesses a manifest advantage over every other kind of Technology in that there is a perfect and sympathetic parallelism between the instructions given and the work to which they are applied. For example, let us imagine the different results in the case of the young Engineer, between a course of simply book technics and a course of actual shop-practice in the use of machine tools. It is clear that the book technics would be nowhere in comparison with the fact teaching of the machines themselves. But in Literary technics, however, we work in a direct way, the illustrations given being identical in nature with the very work the Student is required afterwards to perform, and thence—granted the necessary application—success, in, at all events, a technical sense, is certain.

Only Publishers' Readers, Editors, and the like know

how much many great writers have lost owing to their ignorance, sometimes obstinately wilful, of the technics of the vocation they followed.

Some have been kept back years from the goal of their ambition, because they could not, or would not, conform to system and rule, and probably many a career has been hopelessly frustrated because the young aspirant to honours in Literature, supposed that the possession of what is known as the divine afflatus, would of itself suffice to compel that worldly success which is attained alone by a more or less implicit obedience to certain prescribed rules, and compliance with well-established canons, which care no more for Genius, however great, than the waves did for Canute.

An Engineer must acquire many practical mechanical details of his calling, before anyone will trust him with actual work, a Painter must acquire much purely mechanical knowledge, before his genius, be he ever so gifted, can obtain the smallest public recognition, and the young writer, in like manner, should know as much as *can* be communicated in a Manual of Literary Technology, before he can reasonably expect success in disposing of his intellectual wares.

To every legitimate goal of human ambition there is a safe and well-defined road, and flights " across country," although the steed be a true Pegasus (which is not always the case), almost invariably lead to defeat and shame, and end in the aspirant having eventually to become a pilgrim in the road common to all.

Let no one, especially in these high-pressure competitive times, fall into the capital error of thinking " The Steep where Fame's proud Temple shines afar," is to be stormed by Genius in its crude undisciplined state, unaided by those literary technics which, in their most complete form, can almost match Genius itself, and at all events command worldly success, where Genius alone often achieves only a splendid failure.

As a rule, writers do not care to revert in detail to that painful literary mill through which they have passed. If they give utterance at all to their experience, the subjects selected are such as will attract the general reader, and be popular, and to get practical information from their "Confessions" is very like trying to paint, without first learning how to properly prepare and mix the colours.

There is another point to be considered. The number of writers of all classes is rapidly increasing, with the millions of readers, the natural result of universal education.

In 1884 there were published in the United Kingdom over two thousand newspapers and more than twelve hundred magazines of various kinds, while considerably over one thousand new books issue from the Press yearly.

Obviously with the rapid advance of intellectual culture, the ranks of writers must thicken, and the value in all ways of sound Literary Technics become proportionately enhanced.

Superadded to a more or less natural Literary ability, these Technics will mean all the difference between failure and success, and further still, unquestionably the whole army of Publishers and Editors, and especially their professional advisers, would, indeed, rejoice if the young writer usually approached them with but little of the amateur about him, and with productions which, at all events, fulfilled all the technical requirements of what would be recognised in the Printing Office—that true trial of the Pyx to authors—as legitimate " copy."

The object of this Manual is simply to convey to the reader a clear account of the nature of the indispensable Technics of Literature in its various forms, to warn the young writer of the many pitfalls that beset the initial portion of the Literary career, to show how professional work is actually done, whatever it be, to instruct the reader in the details of " making up " a newspaper, in the *arcana* of Reporting, in the nature of the real, not the fanciful pecuniary return that may be looked for, in these days from Literature, followed as the actual business of life; and especially to explain the mechanical details of the Printing Office so far as they concern writers, and affect the preparation of MSS. designed to reach the Printer's hands.

This naturally includes practical observations on Fiction and other branches of Imaginative Literature, and practical suggestions for acquiring the readiest means, for obtaining the kind of *working* information that is marketable in a Literary sense, and necessarily involves useful hints on the kind of books that should be read with the view of producing the greatest possible Literary effects with the minimum expenditure of time. Then there is the large subject of Journalism to be duly considered, and this includes what is, I believe, not to be found in any other book, viz., a really practical account of the Sub-Editor's duties.

As many authors rise on the Literary ladder from the Sub-Editorial rung thereof, it is a serious omission that no writer has yet condescended to instruct the reader in the mechanical or technical details of the post in a manner easily intelligible to one totally ignorant of the duties involved.

The preparation of MS. or " copy," Publishing, Advertising, and Reviewing of new books, and, in fact, all that concerns the *business* of the general Author or Journalist, in all steps of his career, will be found fully dealt with.

For one considerable class these " Technics " must have a special value.

Already we know instances of ladies employed in Editorial work, outside the sphere of essentially women's publications, and for that numerous class, equipped mentally by Oxford and Cambridge Examinations for Literary work, it must be highly important to have a book of technical Literary reference, in which the reading of a few hours will give them information that has taken the writer many years, and a most varied experience, to acquire.

Those persons who have formed their minds in accordance with the best Ethical schools will, perhaps, allege that my Technics, *per se*, are not the best means fitted for the evolution of the perfect human character contemplated in the philosophy of a Kant or a Fichte.

This may be so, but it may be urged that even authorship is not the highest " evolution " of the human mind and certainly Journalism is not by a long way. Those, however, who have discovered, it matters not how, that they can write, will not, as a rule, assent to the well worn axiom that silence is golden. Articulate they mean to be, in a Literary sense, and all that is claimed for this book is that it will certainly supply them with a course of Literary Technology (not to be obtained in any other book extant), and thus, although they dissent practically from one of

Carlyle's great maxims, they may still conform to the spirit
of his whole teaching, so far as to recognise that *the* road
to true Literary success lies, not in a winged flight
amongst the clouds, but, in steady work, cutting down one
by one, the difficulties that form that terrible forest which,
naturally and necessarily, terrifies the amateur writer,
until the clue is found to every labyrinth.

One word more as to the plan of this Manual. The First
Part is devoted exclusively to the technical consideration
of Book Literature and the Drama, in its intellectual
phases. The Second Part deals with the current aspects
of Journalism and of Periodical writing. A glance at
past Literary history will at once show that the majority
of authors begin and end with the book. The exceptions
prove the rule. Dickens, it is well known at an important
epoch in his wonderful career, tried Journalism, and had
to give it up, and Carlyle—wisely in all probability—
would have nought to do with that special and transitory
form of Literary work.

It must, however, be remembered that we live in times
when even ordinary newspapers are becoming more and
more literary, and good openings are constantly offering in
contemporary Journalism for the purely literary worker,
and thus, in a remarkable degree, apparent enough to any
reflecting observer, the newspaper is constantly tending
more and more to the basis of an unfolded book. It has,
therefore, been deemed well to introduce into the Second
Part a practical account of working Journalism, to define
the main characteristics of the successful working Journalist,
and to describe the practical details of the principal types
of existing periodicals and newspapers, in order that the
young writer may be fortified with all the knowledge

that *can* be acquired without actual personal experience. Obviously, information of the kind here given, will be invaluable to those who may find employment for the first time in these departments, and just as the newspaper is now frequently a book in all but appearance, so will the industrious and skilful newspaper-writer ofttimes find through it his or her appointed path to that great goal of the young writer—the Authorship of Standard Literature.

# II.—POETRY.

*All National Literature originally Poetic—Meaning of the word—The Different Classes of Poetry—The Epic, the Drama, the Lyric, the Hymn, the Ode, the Elegy, the Sonnet. The Structure and Nature of the Sonnet, metre, rhythm, and rhyme, the technics of verse, double and triple rhymes,—Examples—Verse making as an Art—Intellectual v. Sensuous Poetry, errors to be avoided by young verse-writers, imitating the faults of standard poets, Byron, Example of rhetorical rubbish—Childe Harold. Poetic Statistics—Longfellow—Observations on his genius, closing words.*

AS the germ of all national Literature, barbarous or classical, is cast in a poetic mould—even Legislation frequently appearing first in the guise of song of some kind, it has ever been that, with few exceptions, young writers—and certainly those gifted with Fancy or Imagination—find for their initial essays in composition, a rhythmical expression, and in other words, the most usual exposition of the young writer is in verse, approximating more or less to true poetry, according as he or she, may possess some of those virtually indefinable powers, qualities, instincts, and mysterious intuitions, which in their fulness constitute the poet.

Before proceeding further in this connection, a word on Poetry as an Art will be here in place.

Etymologically, Poetry is derived from the Greek *Poico* to make, but the other Greek equivalent *Poiesis* was always applied exclusively to that in which some form of Art in the sense of beauty, sensuous or intellectual, was blended or embodied.

In the Greek mind, Poetry and Art, meant practically the same thing, and thus regarded, true Poetry is not necessarily verse or rhyme. Some prose is infinitely more poetic than verse and good verse too, and many of the writings of Jeremy Taylor, Hooker, Rousseau, Burke, Carlyle, Hawthorne, Emerson, and particularly John Ruskin, are practically poems, although wanting in the mere verbal form.

Conventionally, Poetry, however, needs the verbal clothing of metre and rhyme or at least the former; and perfect Poetry must undoubtedly be metrical.

The various classes of Poetry are broadly the Epic, the Lyric, the Dramatic, the Hymn, the Ode, the Anthem, the Elegy, the Sonnet, and in addition to these, we have didactic and satirical Poetry.

The Epic, of which the principal examples will at once occur to the reader, comes from the Latin *Epicus* and originally from the Greek *Epos*, a song. An Epic Poem is known as heroic and must narrate some story, real or fictitious, depicting in a grand and lofty style, the achievements of some remarkable personage. The matter of such a work comprehends the incidents, the episodes, the moral and the plot of the narrative.

The form relates to the metre, the style, the rhetorical ornaments and graces introduced, and the like, while the aim is to elevate the morals and fire the hearer (for such works were at first always recited) with a love of courage and glory.

The two great Greek Epics are Homer's *Iliad* and *Odyssey*.

The grandest of the Latin Epics is Virgil's *Æneid*, while the principal Italian Epics are Dante's *Divine Comedy* and Tasso's *Jerusalem Delivered*. Milton's *Paradise Lost* is the last of the great world Epics.

The Lyric kind of Poetry was such as was literally sung to the accompaniment of the harp or lyre, and was greatly cultivated by the ancients. Lyrics, however, may be defined as poetical compositions wherein the poet directly and more or less personally expresses himself. Feeling predominates in it, and the individual emotion of the poet is the prime motor.

The Drama is dealt with in the succeeding section.

The Hymn, strictly speaking, is a poem directly addressed to the Deity in some way, while the Ode is simply a short poem, fit for music of the Lyric cast and especially expressing the feelings of the poet in moments of the highest excitement and when his emotions are most intense.

Technically, too, an Ode consists of verses of unequal length in Stanzas and Strophes. A Verse, is, strictly speaking, *one* line only. It is derived from the Latin *Verto* to turn ; a Couplet consists of two lines rhyming together, a Triplet of three lines, and four or more verses in some way connected by rhymes, make a Stanza.

A Strophe is simply a division in an Ode, a Stanza introduced as a new division, and was so named because the Singers turned in one direction while reciting that portion of the poem, and then turned round and sang the next section which had to be of the same length and was termed the Antistrophe.

Practically, a Strophe is a Stanza.

The Elegy is supposed by some etymologists to come from the Latin *Lugeo* to cry out, or wail, and is essentially a mourning song, or at all events, a composition in metre expressive of sorrow.

Gray's *Elegy in a Country Churchyard* is generally considered to be the most perfect example of the true Elegy in the English language. David's lament, too, over Saul and Jonathan, beginning :

"The beauty of Israel is slain upon thy high places ; "

is perfect in pathos, passion, and true sublimity.

The Sonnet yet remains. It is derived from the Italian *Sonnetta*, and is, strictly defined, a short poem of fourteen lines which should be made up of two stanzas of four verses each, and two of three verses each, the rhymes being interwoven. In other words a true Sonnet consists of two quatrains, each having four lines, and two rhymes each, and of two terzarimas, each with three lines and a single rhyme. The closing six lines may be variously arranged as to rhyme, which is absolutely indispensable in a Sonnet.

The usual plan in English examples, is to rhyme the second and sixth line together, although, sometimes, the couplet is used at the close.

The Sonnet must contain one principal idea and should end with a point after the fashion of a good epigram.

The Sonnet is a beautiful form of Poetry at its best, and may be employed in any kind of style and for any sort of subject.

The writing of Sonnets constitutes a very admirable exercise for the young versifier provided only the canons of its correct construction are strictly observed.

Metre, or measure, is the name given to indicate the properly regulated sequence of the syllables, accented and unaccented, constituting verse. A portic foot must have *one* accented syllable and one or more unaccented syllables.

In English verse, metre depends entirely on accent.

The accents must be made to occur at stated intervals, so as to constitute verbal harmony, and each group of syllables, including an accented syllable, is called a " foot."

Every English metre must contain *one* accented syllable and one or two unaccented. As the accent or stress may be on the first, second, or third syllable, there are for the ordinary purposes of English verse five measures, being two of a dissyllabic and three of a tri-syllabic kind as shown in the words :

Hòlly, Revòke, Tèrribly, Renèwal, Galilèe.

These severally correspond to the classic metres known as the Trochee (Hòlly), Iambus (Revòke), Dactyl (Tèrribly), Amphibrach (Renèwal), and Anapaest (Galilèe).

These metres must be arranged in verses ranging from one to many accented syllables, and if short and long lines are introduced in the same composition, a harmony must be maintained, and, above all things, monotony should be avoided.

The time or movement of the metre, must, of course, be suited to the subject, and this is usually an instinctive thing with the writer, as it would be at once felt that a gay measure like that suited for lively, mirthful, brisk pieces would never do for an Elegy.

The rhythm of verse corresponds to the disposition of tones in music.

It is a timed movement, or regulated succession of recurring sounds. It has been said, and justly too, that it is a necessity for man that all sustained movements must be in harmony with a law of musical interchange, and it is on this principle that the sound-undulations constituting verse are regulated and made to form cadences.

It has even been said that the cause of this necessity may be found in the structure and functions of the human constitution, both physiologically and psychologically.

Then, again, it is instinctively perceived that in order that the many parts of any metrical piece may constitute an agreeable whole, those parts must be harmonised together, and hence Poetry imperatively demands a certain harmonious sequence of correlated forms for its proper verbal expression.

Rhyme, which should be written *Rime*, comes, it is said, from the German *Reihen*, to array, and in Anglo-Saxon *Rim-Craeft* signifies to number.

It means technically the recurrence of similar sounds at stated intervals.

These resemblances are various. Thus when words begin with the same consonant, the result is *alliteration* and this was the nearest approximation to what is now know as Rhyme in early Teutonic or Saxon Poetry.

In Spanish there is a kind of Rhyme known as *Assonance*, consisting in the coincidence of the vowels in the corresponding syllables, but this is ineffectual in English, essentially a consonantal language.

Broadly speaking, Rhyme properly means the correspondence in the final syllables of the words closing a verse.

In French verse, perfect identity in each part makes what is termed rich rhyme, as in modèle, fidèle.

In English verse these complete coincidences are no rhymes at all.

"Deplore" does not rhyme with "explore." The vowel and whatever follows it—if anything—must be exactly alike in both, but the articulation before the determining vowel must be different, thus "mark" rhymes perfectly with "arc," "bark," and the like, but not with "remark."

Similarity in spelling does not suffice, as plough is no rhyme to enough.

In double rhymes the *whole* of the unaccented syllables must be identical, a thing often neglected by careless versifiers, and the sound, not the spelling, must be the true guide, as rhymes are to address the ear and not simply the eye, as we might imagine from the wretched attempts at verbal music which distinguish some verse-makers.

In triple rhymes, for example, the correspondence must be absolutely identical in sound in the unaccented portion of the syllables.

The English language, unlike the Italian, does not generally lend itself easily to double or triple rhymes, although, when these can be well accomplished, they are very effective, and form a pleasing and musical variation on the use of single rhymes.

This is an example of double rhyming :

> *Suffering purified thee, such is*
> *Oft its transmutating power,*
> *That the earthly weed it touches,*
> *Turns into a heavenly flower !*

C

In triple rhymes, the following is a type:

*Waving still the flag on high,*
 *Singly there he faced the foe—*
*Who can tell the agony*
 *Felt by those who watched below ?*

As to variations of accepted metres and forms of stanzas—both too numerous to define here—the young verse-maker can soon strike out new lines for himself, provided he always keeps really good models before him, and rigorously subjects each line to the canons of a pure and refined taste.

Verse-making merely considered as an exercise in composition, has very decided utility. If carefully pursued with a true desire to excel, there is no better preparation, perhaps, for really effective, fluent prose.

Very early the verse-maker learns, or should do so, if right principles be adopted as the only guide, to avoid all tautological forms of expression, to eliminate from his compositions redundancies, to make each added expression go straight to the mark, and at last, to find out the true meaning of the golden rule that whatever else may be needed to constitute poetry, it is essential that the conditions laid down include the best words and no more, in the right places.

Poetry may, perhaps, be conveniently divided into two great divisions; that which is chiefly intellectual, and that which is chiefly sensuous.

Of course, these strangely interpenetrate each other, but still the broad distinction named will be found useful.

Intellectual and spiritual poetry naturally go together, and are found exemplified in such perfect types as Pope's

*Essay on Man,* and Milton's *Paradise Lost ;* while the sensuous school is found in Anacreon, to a considerable extent
in Horace, and, coming to our own time, in Swinburne.

Sensuous poetry is eminently realistic, and it may be, so
far as its guiding principles go, fairly well represented as
follows :

> *Its scent and hues the earth renews,*
> *Each season hath its beauty dear ;*
> *The wiser mind will ever find,*
> *Its proper field of action here.*
>
> *Thy thought employ how to enjoy*
> *Of generous Earth its offerings best;*
> *This life is rough, and soon enough*
> *The lips of Death must tell the rest !*

This might be taken as a type of Agnostic poetry.
Material loveliness is its lowest, and material heroism its
highest level ; but we must not look here for "the light that
never was on land or sea, the consecration and the poet's
dream."

Still less is this the spirit which prompted the poet to tell
us of "the longing to something, afar from the sphere of
our sorrow."

The true technics of verse-making—and this is obviously
indispensable as the vehicle of any poetry that may be in
the writer—must be carefully acquired by the preliminary
study of Prosody, which can be learned first of all from
any good English grammar, and then by a catholic course
of poetic reading, and a careful discrimination between the
good, bad, and indifferent things that are to be found in
all poets alike, not excepting Shakespeare, who has some

execrable lines, or Tennyson, who, with all his general finish, has numerous blemishes.

The young verse-maker, too, as a part of his or her training, should acquire a clear understanding of the essential and vital distinctions that underlie the various kinds of poetry, and especially of the contrast between the Classical and the Romantic schools.

In the one, the harmony of each part subordinated to one mighty and overpowering finality, is the end in view; and in the other, the elaboration and enriching of a thousand details with separate gems of thought and fancy, are the guiding principles that are to be followed.

Above all, must the young writer be warned to avoid the common error—fatal to any true progress if persisted in—of moulding his productions on the average, and still more so, on the very inferior phases of Standard Poets.

Every poet, as Edgar Allen Poe eloquently pointed out, in one of his remarkable essays, is essentially unequal, and there is a tendency in the young writer to compare his best lines with the worst of some favourite author. If we always compared, however, such productions with even the better passages of recognised writers, what trash most of the former would at once be seen to be, even by those who were quite ignorant of poetic technics.

The carelessness of great poets has much to answer for in unhappily furnishing precedent for an infinite mass of absolute rubbish.

To take a case in point, the opening stanzas of Byron's *Ode to Saint Helena* are, at the best, but very frothy rhetoric, without even a touch of true poetry, and approaching very close indeed to downright bathos, and the same remark applies to much of his occasional verse, yet this same pen which produced such rubbish as the *Lines to a Tear* in the Hours of Idleness, gave us the pathos and passion of *Childe Harold's Pilgrimage*, and enshrined therein some of the most beautiful gems of pure poetry in the language.

One word more, let the young writer, once he has obtained a mastery over the technics of verse, beware of sinking—as most amateur versifiers do—into the hopeless state of being an unconscious echo of half-remembered poetry floating through the mind in a more or less nebulous way.

Let him look at everything he writes about directly, and not through the form of expression that some one else has employed.

Let him endeavour to perceive the hidden sense and significance of things as they are to him, and not as they have appeared to others, although those "others" be Homer or Shakespeare ; let him strive at all times to go down to the very roots and source of everything, whether it be a part of the objective or the subjective life, and then, and then only, will he be likely to write something that the world will not willingly let die.

And now let us turn for a moment to what, if a rather dry and matter-of-fact consideration, has, nevertheless, its significance and value to the young writer of verse. An eminent firm of publishers—a house issuing, probably, more books than any other single firm in the United Kingdom—furnished some time since, the returns of a year's sales of standard poetry. The following are the figures, giving the number of copies sold of each of the works of the Poets cited :—

Byron, 2,380; Burns, 2,250; Campbell, 207; Chaucer, 637; Cowper, 800; Hemans, 1,900; Hood, 980; Leigh

Hunt, 76; Keats, 40; L. E. L., 109; Longfellow, 6,000; Lowell, 307; Milton, 1850; Moore, 2,276; Poe, 310; Pope, 706; Rogers, 32; Scott, 3,170; Shakespeare, 2700; Shelley, 500; Southey, 267; Spencer, 360.

Now what at first strikes one here is the very obvious fact that, judged by these statistics, the greatest and truest poetry is by no means that in the most demand. Longfellow sells more than twice as well as Byron and Shakespeare, and nearly twice as well as Walter Scott! Keats, who possessed an extraordinary genius, and whose *Endymion* is a permanent addition to English classic poetry, comes out— tried by this booksellers' test—as a miserable failure, and so, too, does Rogers, whose *Pleasures of Memory* was once a universal favourite. Spencer, too, who in this list comes nearest to Shakespeare as an *imaginative* poet, is a failure too. Campbell, once so popular, is even worse!

No doubt the great success of Longfellow is mainly due to three marked characteristics,—he is a remarkably pure writer, he has extreme simplicity, and he rises so very little above the usual range of ordinary sentimental and feeling people, that he unconsciously flatters his readers by producing poetry that many more can write, too, after the way has once been shown!

Longfellow possessed a singular verbal fluency, a very correct metrical ear, and by reason of his extraordinary acquaintance with the poetic literature of the world, had acquired a really wonderful power of most versatile expression. His veins of absolute originality were neither numerous nor rich, but he was a finished master of his art, and his literary career, with its very remarkable triumphs, might, if fully analyzed, well illustrate the main contention of this work, that technics alone—if judiciously applied—

count for very much in all the literary competitions of the day.

Finally, in this place, as one more illustration of the way in which "Homer nods" in the persons of some of our standard authors, we need but cite a few examples more—examples, of course, of what the young writer must carefully avoid.

The author of that splendid, if strangely unequal work, —*The Night Thoughts*—Edmund Young—perpetrated the following verses, which will be found in most editions of his collected poems :—

> "Trade's the source, sinew, soul of all ;
> Trade's all herself, her's, her's the ball ;
> Where most unseen, the goddess still is there,
> Trade leads the dance, trade lights the blaze,
> The courtier's pomp, the student's ease !
> 'Twas Trade at Blenheim fought and closed the war ! "

This is a wretched batch of verses. It is simply hopelessly bad, and was not worth correcting from the first. In the short space, too, of only six lines, it includes two false rhymes,—"there" and "war," and "blaze" and "ease." Then, again, we find Cowper, on such a theme as the loss of the *Royal George*,—in itself a splendid subject for the elegiac muse—producing the following lines which are actually included among his "poems":—

> "A land breeze shook the shrouds,
> And she was overset,
> Down went the 'Royal George,'
> With all her crew complete ! "

A child of eight or nine might do better than this; and

both Chatterton and Mrs. Hemans did better things at that age.  Here, again, notice the defective character of the rhyme.  With regard to finished rhyme, it is worthy of notice that, strictly speaking, the consonantal portion should be varied, and in a stanza, for example, closing, say the first and third lines with such rhymes as "sound" and "crown'd," which are perfect, the second and fourth lines should not close with "mind" and "find," or any like combination, but with something entirely different, phonetically speaking, as "day" and "may," or "like" and "strike."  The same principle applies to a sequence of couplets.  Thus in Byron's exquisite monologue, *The Prisoner of Chillon*, the following passage occurs :—

> "Avoiding only as I trod,
>  My brothers' graves without a sod;
>  For if I thought, with heedless tread,
>  My step profaned their lowly bed,
>  My breath came gaspingly and thick,
>  And my crushed heart felt blind and sick."

In the above it had been better to avoid such rhymes as "tread" and "bed,"—perfect in themselves, however, —immediately after the similar sounds, "trod" and "sod." These are delicate points often missed by writers of real genius, but it may be assumed as certain that whoever carefully attends to such points of finish, will reap a sure reward thence, and will gain immensely in originality, precisely as a diamond of even the first water, does when cut to the utmost attainable refractive advantage.

These remarks are thrown out rather as hints and suggestions, than as dogmas.  It is hoped that they may induce young writers to take less for granted, and to enquire for

themselves into the Reason why, of all that is put before
them by the printer as " poetry." The writer who com-
pares his or her verses with the pieces found in Byron's
*Hours of Idleness* is not at all likely to do such good work
as a writer who selects for a style and standard, the best
portions of *Childe Harold*.

It is worth while to contrast two representative passages
here from both sources :—

In the *Hours of Idleness* we are told that,

" The man doom'd to sail with the blast of the gale,
 Through billows Atlantic to steer,
As he bends o'er the wave which may soon be his grave,
 The green sparkles bright with a tear."

This is from *Childe Harold*, and relates to the field of
Marathon :—

" The sun, the soil, but not the slave, the same,
 Unchanged in all, except its foreign lord,
 Preserves alike its bounds and boundless fame,
 The battle-field, where Persia's victim horde,
 First bow'd beneath the brunt of Hellas' sword,
 As on that morn to distant glory dear,
 When Marathon became a magic word
 Which utter'd, to the hearer's eye appear
The camp, the host, the fight, the conqueror's career."

Observe the difference. Here in the last excerpt we
have unmistakably, power, and that firm grasp of reality
which infects the reader with the mood of the writer;
there is consummate art, but it is wholly concealed. The
opening verse, composed entirely of very simple words
only, is highly instructive as showing how great an effect

*can* be produced by the common words of every-day speech, while the *cumulative* effect of each line in the stanzas, from the opening to the close, is worth careful study. One more instance, although from a poet of much lower rank, but one who is a master of the technics of his art, may here be cited.

In his beautiful poem, *After Flodden*, the survivor of those who rescued the Scottish Royal Banner is made to say— by Professor Aytoun—on his return to mourning Edinburgh :—

> " Take the banner that I give you—
> Guard it as a holy thing—
> For the stain you see upon it—
> Is the life-blood—of your—king ! "

How simple, but how direct, how powerful and how pathetic !

Another example of poetry of this Homeric cast is to be found in the same writer in reference to the Battle of Killiecrankie (July 27, 1689), where " brave Dundee mid faint huzzas expired," as another bard has somewhat inaccurately sung, for the Marquis, did not die *on* the battle-field.

In the lines referred to, however, dealing with the critical moment when the hidden Highlanders suddenly poured forth on Mackay's little army, as it unconcernedly entered the dangerous defile, the poet exclaims :

> " Bursting from the rocky ridges
> Swept the hurricane of steel,—
> Peel'd the Slogan of MacDonald,
> Flash'd the broadsword of Lochiel ! "

I have said above that the young verse-maker should, above all things, strive to look at Nature through his own eyes, and not through those of other people, however great they be.

How different, in this respect, is a poet like Gray from Wordsworth! When the latter tells us that "the daisy, by the shadow that it casts, protects the lingering dewdrop from the sun," we feel instinctively that the writer sees with his own, and not with borrowed, eyes; but when, even in Gray's famous *Elegy*, we read:

"The curfew tolls the knell of parting day
    The lowing herd winds slowly o'er the lea,
The ploughman homeward plods his weary way,
    And leaves the world to darkness and to me—"

it at once strikes the thoughtful mind that this is more the poetry of epithet than of nature, and it could be written by one whose knowledge of rural sights and sounds was derived entirely from books. It is curious, by the way, while on this subject, what a piece of literary patch-work this famous poem really is—a poem owing much of its fame to the happy circumstance that it appeared during a period by no means prolific of true poetry.

Thus we read:

"And all the air a solemn stillness holds
    Save where the beetle wheels his *droning* flight,—"

This, surely, is very like the passage in *Macbeth*:

"The shard-born beetle with his *drowsy* hum
    Hath rung Night's peal,—"

while in the beautiful *Ode to Evening* of Collins we find:

> " Or, where the beetle winds
>     His small but sullen horn "—

Then, after telling us that

> " Beneath the rugged elms
>     The rude forefathers of the hamlet sleep " —

Gray says :—

> " The breezy call of incense breathing morn,
>     The swallows' twittering from the straw-built shed,
> The cock's shrill clarion, and the echoing horn,
>     No more shall rouse them from their lowly bed."

Surely this is but an echo from Pope's *Messiah* :

> " With all the incense of the breathing Spring."

Line two seems strangely like a verse from Thomas Kidd, a forgotten Elizabethan writer, who sings of :

> " The wandering swallow with her broken wing,"

while Milton has :

> " The crested cock whose clarion sounds
>     The silent hours "—

The line, so much admired,

> " The paths of glory lead but to the grave,"

is surely but a half poetic truth. Do they not beckon on enthusiastic youth to all time ? Campbell, also, writing of the fallen patriot, declares that he is not dead whose glorious mind lifts ours on high, adding the well-known lines :

" To live in hearts we leave behind
   Is *not* to die ! "

The famous stanza :

" Full many a gem of purest ray serene,
   The dark unfathomed caves of ocean bear,
Full many a flower is born to blush unseen,
   And waste its sweetness on the desert air,"

is more beautiful than original ; for, in Milton's *Comus*, we
find the following :

" That like to rich and various gems inlay
   The unadorned bosom of the deep."

Pope, too, sings of—

" Roses that in deserts bloom and die,"

and, in Chamberlayne's *Pharonida*, we have the following :

" Like beauteous flowers which vainly waste their scent
   Of odours in unhaunted deserts."

Finally, one stanza of this splendid poem is ungrammatical :—

" Their name, their years, spelt by the unlettered Muse,
   In place of Fame and Elegy supply,
And many a holy text around she strews
   That teach the rustic moralist to die."

Teach should, surely, be *teaches*, and the mistake might
have been easily avoided by writing :

" And many holy text*s* around she strews
   That teach the rustic moralist to die."

It is possible enough that all these coincidences may be merely accidental, but the truth they point to is that the poet should look at man and nature *direct*, and not through the medium of books. If we were to analyse the details of Shelley's *Ode to the Skylark*, it would be impossible to find for its special beauties a like list of parallel passages in all the wide range of poetic literature.

# III.—FICTION.

*Its Functions and Utility—Importance of Literary Technics to the Novelist—Crude Work—A Glance at the History of Story Telling as an Art—The Contemporary Novel—How to Work—The Way to Success in Fiction—Examples—New Openings—Charles Reade—Statistics of Fiction—Novel Writing Reduced to an Art.*

STRICTLY speaking—if we follow in a precise sequence the growth of the human mind in its literary expressions—the Drama, rude and uncultured, would properly take its due place in the van. But somewhat ahead of the Drama—at first little more than a dialogue with metrical variations—would come Poetry, and as the consolidation of many poetic forms, we reach through a long series of legends, romances, and fictitious narratives, the contemporary novel, which, as the fruition of so many literary forms, has itself become diversified in a most remarkable degree. In the present work, however, which is obviously meant to aid specially those who are engaged in, or contemplating, the production of Fiction, I place the Novel immediately after the Poem—and in truth there is, as every thoughtful student must perceive, a close connection, and a subtle affinity, between these two principal forms of literary expression, which outside the well defined ranks of actually useful or technical books, compose the principal mass of Literature in its most permanent and popular forms.

Amongst the salient "evolutions" of contemporary Literature, indeed, the novelist is constantly growing more important, popular and prominent. The writer of Fiction, at the best, is really our domestic annalist, and as the exponent of Society in its most kaleidoscopic aspects, subserves a most useful purpose, and does much, undoubtedly, to form and colour the social culture of the day. The prizes, too, increase in number as the circle of readers of various classes constantly multiply and widen, and although, as of old, it is given only to a fortunate and gifted few to attain the most commanding positions, there is always ample encouragement in this department for writers of but moderate ability, provided only they possess great power of reproducing what they see and hear, and, in addition to industry, have that correct taste and sound judgment which will enable them, so to speak, to edit themselves. In truth, if the number of really first-rate works of Fiction remains still limited as ever, the multiplying of good books of the second rank goes on with amazing rapidity, and indicates that there must be a large number of separate fiction reading circles, within which shine, with more or less splendour, sundry bright particular stars whose rays, nevertheless, do not reach the great reading world viewed as a whole.

How much we owe to the novelist, even of the second rank, will be perceived if we only reflect on the vast influence that Fiction can exercise on the great body of the nation. For one thing, the novelist is a social cicerone, and although the pictures drawn may be more or less exaggerated and even erroneous, on the whole the writer of fiction is a more or less faithful photographer and reporter of that domestic life which, when well delineated, has such irresistible attractions for the normal British mind. Of course I am here referring to the domestic novel pure and simple, which now forms the staple of English fiction, and round which cluster innumerable varieties of story telling or character painting, from the detective like tales of Mr. Wilkie Collins to the almost Shakespearean dramas of George Elliot.

To many among us, too, environed by hard monotonous realities of work-a-day life, cut off by stern circumstances from mixing freely among their fellow creatures, and thus enlarging their sympathetic capacities, the novelist is, indeed, a blessing, lifting them, for a season, out of their dark and dreary lives, and teaching them that their own little, narrow, selfish spheres do not comprehend the true diapason of human life. To many among us, too, the novelist's pages give the only glimpses obtainable of the manners and customs, and the only echoes that can be had of the circles beyond and above, or it may be, below them, and, in such a materialistic matter-of-fact age as ours, it is in the novel chiefly that ethical teachings and the spirit of sentiment are found.

Such in truth are some of the high and truly useful functions of the novelist, and in a treatise like this, dealing with Literature in its widest contemporary sense, it is obviously in place to address some words of advice and of caution to those who find their literary bias lies decidedly in the direction of Fiction.

It is in the experience of every Publisher's Reader, and increasingly so, to find an enormous amount of real ability

D

and, now and then, even some genius of the narrative or dramatic type, utterly wasted and rendered futile in the writer's productions, owing simply to that crudity and want of a true sense of intellectual proportion which usually marks the early efforts of young writers of both sexes, and which might be entirely obviated by the simple agency of a little technical knowledge, and the possession of a fairly correct taste. Both knowledge and taste are the results of study and that mental discipline which normally springs out of self-culture, and these are to be attained only at the cost of more or less application, and especially by the acquisition of a fairly exhaustive knowledge of Fiction viewed historically. Hard reading and exact thinking can alone result in easy and yet forcible writing, and for want of the requisite intellectual training what lamentable shortcomings, and how many examples of downright ignorance are found in much of the published fiction of the day. " Well," reply some aspirants for literary honours, " after all these stories *are* published ! " Yes ; but just reflect on those, some of which may be far superior in originality, that utterly fail to pass the ordeal of the Publisher's literary advisers, solely consequent on gross errors of form, solecisms, and the betrayal by the writer of gross ignorance of, perhaps, the fundamental laws of the art.

It is in no way my business to make story-tellers, nor would it be possible so to do by any kind of written instructions, but given the faculty for narrating, or in some way of reproducing the phases of human life, it is clear that the addition thereto of sound literary technics must in themselves constitute to the writer an additional power, one that cannot fail most effectively to enhance the value of whatever natural literary ability may exist.

Fiction is the oldest, probably, strictly speaking, the earliest of literary *arts, i.e.,* fiction dealing more or less with truth under various more or less transparent disguises. No art was more simple in its origin, and none has become more complex in its ultimate forms.

Let us, for a moment, so far as is practicable in a very limited space, survey the whole field of Fiction historically.

The earliest examples known of prose fiction are the famous Milesian tales ascribed to Aristides. The Milesians were some Ionic Greeks, who settled in Asia Minor, and fell under the Persian yoke in 494, B.C. These tales have all perished, but some forty stories by Parthenius Niceas, are generally believed to be adaptations thence. In Greece itself prose romance did not appear until after the days of Alexander the Great, and thus there was imparted to the first rude forms of European fiction a decided Eastern tinge, and a variety of incidental " properties," if we may so call it, from the Orient. Clearchus, a pupil of Aristotle and Antonius Diogenes, the author of *Ta hyper Thoulen Apista*—(incredible things beyond Thule) —are two capital examples, and were laid under heavy contributions by Achilles Tatius many centuries later. After a long interval—for the novelist of those remote times was but little encouraged according to contemporary criteria—came Lucian, who flourished during the reign of Marcus Antonius; Lucian, however, was really a humourist and satirist in story-teller guise, and was a kind of classic. Rebelais Iamblichus and Heliodorus succeeded as romance writers; the latter was a Christian novelist, and his loves of *Theagenes and Charicleia* is considered the most ancient erotic romance extant. This old classic work, by the way, sometimes ingeniously likened to Richardson's style of writing, has been greatly drawn on by various modern writers, and has sometimes been actually copied in part verbatim. Then came Longus with his *Daphnis,* and Chloe, the type of the pastoral tale, and after him we have Chariton, from one of whose erotic romances it is thought that Shakespeare derived the leading incidents in *Romeo and Juliet.* It will be observed that but few names cover a long period, and a student of the principal erotic romance of the classic or pagan period and the dark ages, immediately succeeding them, will find that the various stories have little of what is now understood as *plot.* They generally abound in incident, but usually the interest pivots on the separation, by violence, of hero and heroine, and their respective adventures and trials in seeking to meet again. The *Deus ex Machina* is largely used, and magic, in more or less ingenious forms, is made to conceal the want of true invention in the writers. Before leaving the early classic period we must not omit to refer to Appuleius, who wrote a strange fantastic fiction called the *Ass,* wherein are related the adventures of a young man metamorphosed into that animal. This story, known as the *Golden Ass,* was very popular during the Middle Ages, and supplied Boccaccio with much of his material, and later on was pilfered from by the author of *Gil Blas.* The *Ass* contains, by the way, the beautiful episode of *Cupid and Psyche,* and this is undoubtedly the loveliest and purest piece of fiction that the Ancient World has given us.

Romantic fiction in Western Europe had two strong and special sources for its inspiration, the one the rude, but on the whole manly and even heroic mythology of the Norse and kindred warrior peoples ; and the other the far more varied and intricate legend and story of those oriental races, who, after the complete destruction of the remains of Roman Dominion, were brought through the agency of the Crusades into close contact with the new and ardent chivalry of Gothic Europe. A third source of inspiration too, may be found as special to our land, in the Keltic races of Britain, and in the myths of early British heroes like Arthur, while France, in the tales of Charlemagne and his Paladins gave the world a series of stories which served as stock themes for many weavers of mediæval romance, and became ultimately crystallized in such works as *Amadis de Gaul.* About the period of the Fifteenth and Sixteenth Centuries one Raoul le Febre marked a new departure in fiction by reproducing in knightly guise, and with all proper feudal surroundings, the heroes of antiquity, and thence we have such monstrous productions as *Jason and Medea,* where Jason is an armed knight, and all kinds of liberties are taken with the most respectable Pagans of the Classical Dictionary. Italy did not, so far as is known, contribute to fiction proper until the Thirteenth Century, the earliest work at all answering to the novel being the *Cento Novelle Antiche,* and this of unknown authorship, was succeeded by the *Decameron,* which marks, perhaps, the first true epoch in the history of later fiction. But meanwhile a series of spiritual romances—the rude originals of the modern religious novels —were being put forth as " an unobjectionable literature," sometimes by priests and monks, and included with these is the greatest of them all—the *Legenda Aurea*—the *Golden Legend.*

During the Sixteenth and Seventeenth Centuries fiction began to crystallize and to assume several distinct forms, most of which have been more or less preserved ever since. Thus we have during this later period the comic romance—of which the great example is Rabelais; the political romance—type—Sir Thomas More's *Utopia;* the pastorial romance—types—Sannazzaro's *Arcadia,* Montemayor's *Diana,* and Sir Philip Sydney's *Arcadia;* the heroic romance—types, the *Dissensions of the Zegris and the Abencerrages,* and the many romances of Madame de Scuderi. These works were intolerably tedious and extremely affected, and were ultimately withered into well-deserved oblivion by the satire of Molière and Boileau.

Reaching the Eighteenth Century, we find the two nations really great in fiction are England and France. There were sundry very popular but highly objectionable weavers of stories in the reign of Charles II., but the father of the English novel is undoubtedly De Foe, and after him—how great a contrast!—ranks Richardson. Then follow many writers, including the mighty Fielding, and after the coarseness of a materialistic age, wanting all true refinement, had culminated in a Sterne, Goldsmith, with the *Vicar of Wakefield,* marked the purer phase for the English novel. An interval then succeeded, and the next phase was introduced by Horace Walpole with his *Castle of Otranto,* and a new era of wild romance, tricked out with mediæval splendour set in. Clara Reeve with the *Old English Baron,* and Mrs. Radcliffe, won for the times enormous popularity, and it was only when writers like William Godwin produced strong vivid pictures of contemporary life, that the romantic era began to go out of fashion only to be resuscitated later on by the genius of Sir Water Scott, and later still by the consummate art of the late Lord Lytton.

In France, Marivaux, the Abbé Prevot, and Rousseau,

were the great lights of serious and sentimental fiction, while in humorous and satirical romance, we have Le Sage, Crebillon Diderot, and last, but not least, Voltaire.

Cervantes must be paragraphed alone. His great work is not so much a novel as a literature of its own, and his far-reaching influence did not exhaust itself for several generations.

In Germany the novel as shown in the imaginative genius of Wieland, Jean Paul Richter, De la Motte Fouqué, Ludwig Tieck, Hoffmann, Schiller, and greatest of all, Goethe, has always taken a more distinctly poetic cast than in England and France, and the true source probably of our own philosophic novels is to be found in the metaphysical romances of the Fatherland. The novelists of the present century are far too numerous to be particularised here. Their names are legion, and the great ones of Europe, including Russia and America, form a host of themselves.

The contemporary novel, the natural birth of all the great periods so slightly sketched above, is a thing entirely *sui generis.* It may, therefore, seem to some a simple waste of time to study the past, but in these fiercely competitive days it will always be found that, other things being equal, that writer will succeed the most of all who is the best versed in the annals of ancient fiction and romance. Exceptions, there are no doubt, like Dickens, who, however, was himself, at all times, a laborious student of literature, but the rule holds good that the man or woman who attempts anything of fiction in these days without first being really cultured in a clear knowledge of what others have done, cannot reasonably expect to succeed greatly. Book culture should go hand in hand with careful observation of human nature itself, and so far as practicable of still life. The writer of fiction would do well to regard the art as one of painting, with words for pigments, and remember he has the enormous advantage over the painter of an infinitely greater variety of shades, colors, and of forms.

There, undoubtedly, is an enormous and an ever increasing public for all kinds of contemporary fiction, but the public standard insensibly rises, and works which would in 1850 have earned a solid reputation, hardly obtain a place in the third class in 1880. This is the secret of what publishers and booksellers tell us with regard to even such literary giants as Walter Scott. The *Woman in White* is by no means a great fiction; it is wanting in every true element of that greatness which exists in such a novel as *Jane Eyre,* but it struck out distinctly *new* lines of plot and invention, and, above all things, in these high pressure times of over tasked lives and jaded brains, do the masses of readers, like the Athenians of St. Paul's days, seek a new thing.

This is the true reason why Publishers set their faces so ruthlessly against the historic romance, such a favourite form of fiction with amateur writers. An historic romance is not likely, every Publisher or reader knows perfectly well, to be better than *Ivanhoe* or *Harold*, and if it were as good as either of those splendid works, the general public would care little for a *tour de force* reputation of the character which formerly fascinated the majority of readers. G. P. R. James was once extremely popular, and most of his novels are examples of fairly good literary workmanship, but none of them, if published now as new works, would command many readers. We have in this craving for something new the key to the extraordinary success of Zola in France, and it is probably in Realism only that great and fortune-making successes in the art of Fiction will be attained.

This is not high art. There will be at all times a cultured public willing to read thoughtful, philosophical Fiction, but the writers able to supply that demand must not look for sudden popularity nor great pecuniary returns. In this as in other matters of our higher and nobler life, the purer forms of art must be of themselves the writer's incorruptible and enduring reward.

And now passing to another consideration, it must be confessed that the complexities of our advancing and very material civilization do and will offer extraordinary openings for the contemporary writer of Fiction. It is equally obvious that except in special cases of an unusual disposition of the creative Imagination, the Past will be less and less utilised by novelists. That the mental training requisite to properly equip the successful popular novelist must be increasingly wide, catholic, and deep, goes without saying. The writer who aspires to a high place in the world of Fiction must practically know something of every science and art and especially know where and how really complete knowledge can be obtained as often as a profound acquaintance with some specific subject is needed by the exigencies of plot, situation, still life, conversation and character delineation. That many successful novels appear by writers whose ignorance is equally conspicuous with their natural talent, is no true encouragement to the slip shod and superficial novelist. Such half successes will gradually but surely in such a high pressure competitive age as this become more and more infrequent and the day is at hand when even in the charmed regions of pure Imagination, technic literary skill will be indispensable to ensure anything like solid success.

It is, of course, understood that no amount of technics, or of the most careful and honest self-culture can *per se,* create a novelist, but granted only what may be conveniently called a natural talent for narration or for auto-biographical story telling only—then, the addition in good season of a system of literary technics must surely tell enormously in favour of the writer. Unquestionably famous writers have won fame and even fortune, who would have scorned the notion that a novelist should be trained for work like a candidate for competitive examinations, but even these lofty geniuses would have attained to far higher renown had they laboured under that earnest spirit which inspired Horace when he produced that masterpiece—the *Ars Poetica*—and it will invariably be found if we inquire closely into the real facts, that, as Pope assures us :

" True ease in writing comes from art not chance."

It is manifestly not the province of this Treatise to lay down any set of rules to guide the young novelist, but it is quite legitimate and practicable, to offer hints and suggestions, and especially to caution him or her, against those fatal facilities of the inexperienced pen, which insures the rejection of so many MSS., and the utter waste of enormous toil, to say nothing of heart sickening disappointments.

In general, to weave fancies, the writer should have a good knowledge of facts. If we critically examine the

highest examples of descriptive poetry for instance, it will
become at once apparent that the Poet had an exact and
thorough knowledge of the subjects wherewith he has dis-
ported with such consummate art. The most common
and most serious fault of the young writer is, unconsciously,
to give pale reflexes of his favourite writers, a fault surely
avoided by going, as they did, to fact and nature. Never
describe a description, nor echo the verbal melody of
another. In describing persons, places, or things, let the
work be direct and personal, and if, as the exigencies of
narrative sometimes demand, places are to be described,
unknown to the writer, then "get up" the subject from
good, solid, trustworthy writers, the drier the better, so
they are good, as that will prevent them from having
become popular reading, and thus greatly increase the
verisimilitude of a clever and fluent transcript thence.
Strive on all occasions to describe, however, from direct
*personal* observation. This, indeed, is the only certain way
to impart reality and resultant force to writing. Never
rack the memory to recall the fine things that others have
said or sung about any of the phases of the natural world,
but view them steadfastly yourself, and then reproduce
your own mental impression in the fewest possible, and the
shortest and simplest words. You can always "touch up,"
as a skilful painter does, afterwards, if need be, and it is
surprising how firm a hold on the reader the writer has
who trains his apprehensive faculties into a kind of mirror
to reflect exactly the aspects of still life and the phases of
the human nature within his ken.

Everyone, who has read much of the crude work of
young and ill-trained writers, knows how prone they are to
liken their characters to something else. Figures of

speech indeed, are with them, plentiful as commas, and the heroine is always like a lily, or the snow, the swan, or the dove ; or her nails are like sea shells, or her eyes like violets, and in a word the descriptions are smothered in fragments of flowers of poetic speech culled from all the best remembered and favourite authors of the writer.

It is thus, too often, that all firm grasp of realism is lost, and the unhappy writer naturally fails to impress the reader, simply because he is himself a copyist of a picture or the echo of a sound of which the world has already probably had enough.

Space here is necessarily limited, or numberless instances could be cited, and from print too, of utterly worthless writing of this kind, and as we all know, there are numbers of stereotyped matters belonging to Imaginative Literature which like the Upas Tree that once grew in so many youthful poems, ought never to be seen in any composition that rises above the school exercise level.

As an important and indeed invaluable addition to the reading of Fact—books of all kinds, the systematic cutting out and properly indexing in books, of extraordinary occurrences of every kind that are reported in newspapers, would be of essential service.

By doing this in a few years the careful student will accumulate an astonishing collection of authenticated examples of the well-worn saying that Truth *is* stranger than Fiction.

The meaning of this paradox may be, perhaps, clear to some when it is remembered that the *best* Fiction is necessarily the closest approximation to Truth itself.

The late Charles Reade was a striking instance of the sterling money and fame value to be found in the patient collection of contemporary facts, and it would astound some if they knew how little, comparatively speaking, that great writer owed of incidents merely to his invention, and how much to his judicious and patient industry.

It will be useful and interesting in this place to note as suggestive of the general contemporary appreciation of Fiction some statistics actually furnished by Messrs. Routledge, who print nearly six millions of books of Fiction in a year.

Taking the sales of a single year we have the following, relative to what may be called Standard Novelists :

Lytton's (sixpenny edition), 80,000 ; Scott's Novels, 30,000 ; Marryat's Novels, 60,000 ; *Robinson Crusoe* (18 *months*), 40,000 ; *The English Opium-eater*, 1,910 ; *Gulliver's Travels*, 2,480 ; *Jack Hinton*, 8,000 ; Sterne, 2,865 ; *Innocents Abroad*, 5,575 ; *Arabian Nights*, 1,403 ; *Æsop's Fables*, 2,427 ; *Amelia*, 4,900 ; *Joseph Andrews*, 5,250 ; *Tom Jones*, 8,200.

Of the late Lord Lytton's Works at a higher price there were sold in a single year :

*Night and Morning*, 1,170 ; *The Last of the Barons*, 1,440 : *The Last Days of Pompeii*, 1,470 ; *Alice*, 980 ; *The Caxtons*, 880 ; *Pelham*, 656 ; *A Strange Story*, 740 ; *What Will He Do with it ?* 1,604 ; *Eugene Aram*, 870 ; *My Novel*, 700.

Coming to a far lower type of Fiction the following figures are given as a twelve months' sale of Harrison Ainsworth's novels :

*Windsor Castle*, 10,170 ; *Tower of London*, 11,750 ; *Rookwood*, 9,256 ; *Old St. Paul's*, 10,000 ; *Jack Sheppard*, 8,400 ; *Guy Fawkes*, 9,880 ; *Lancashire Witches*, 5,950.

Turning to another writer—an undoubted master of the story telling art, Fenimore Cooper, we have the subjoined results :

*The Deerslayer*, 3,290 ; *The Bravo*, 1,550 ; *The Borderers*, 2,030 ; *The Last of the Mohicans*, 4,360 ; *The Pathfinder*, 3,636 ; *The Pilot*, 3,575 ; *Prairie*, 3,200 ; *Red Rover*, 2,830. .

These returns are entirely eclipsed, however, by Alexandre Dumas. For we find that of *Monte Christo*, published in two parts, the number sold was in a single year 41,160 ; of *Twenty Years After*, 10,290 ; of *The Three Musketeers*, 11,100. This is far ahead of Eugène Sue, of whose *Mysteries of Paris* a year's sale is only 3,400, and *The Wandering Jew*, 2,080 copies, while of Victor Hugo's *Notre Dame*, only 4,530 copies were sold. Two other popular books are *Handy Andy* and *Valentine Vox*, of the first of which one year's sale was over 18,000, and of the second 14,000 copies.

The returns relative to Charles Dickens will no doubt strike the reader as low, but it should be remembered that the books of the great master of humorous fiction were, so to speak, long since in the homes of the people, and the figures cited below of a year's sales are relatively high. They are :

*American Notes*, 3,345 ; *Barnaby Rudge*, 6,260 ; *Grimaldi*, 3,266 ; *Nicholas Nickleby*, 6,670 ; *Pickwick*, 7,650 ; *Sketches by Boz*, 4,060 ; *Oliver Twist*, 5,456 ; *Old Curiosity Shop*, 7,000.

At the opening of this chapter it is stated that the novel is certainly one of the oldest of literary forms, although its existing shape, within a most varied range, has been more or less defined, only some three centuries or so. That there is an art of Poetry is universally admitted, and it was as well or better understood by the Greeks and Romans than by ourselves, but the notion of an art of

Fiction is not quite so popular, although well understood
by all true students of the business of Novel-making. The
general technical views of the writer in regard to the production of the Novel on a certain basis and in some conformity to certain definite canons of construction, were fully
formulated *before* they received a very gratifying confirma-
tion by a writer in the *Times*, who, in a leading article on
Novels and Novel-writers, wrote as follows:

"Is there an art of fiction? Can we, if we please, found
an academy, institute lectures, receive pupils, and teach
them how to tell stories? It is claimed by one who is himself a story-teller that it is as possible to teach fiction as to
teach painting; that both arts are governed by certain
laws and rules which may be taught; that there is a *technique* which may be taught; that there are models which
may be studied; masters whose methods may be learned
and imitated, general elementary rules which may be
laid down; in fact, that so far as any art can be taught,
fiction may be taught, and so far as it is desirable to
have art schools, it is desirable to teach the art of
fiction. On the other hand, it is not contended that every
one can be taught to write a novel any more than that
every one may learn how to paint a portrait or carve a
group in marble. But provided that one is born with the
story-telling faculty, the art of fiction may be taught, it is
urged, with as much certainty and quickness as any other
art. If it is argued that people learn this art without
instructors, professors, or course of lectures, the reply is
that if they had previously gone through such a 'mill' as
is provided for students in painting, they would have
learned how to write novels without the disastrous failures
which too often attend early efforts, without the waste of

that valuable material which is never so fresh and good as when the novelist first begins, and without the acquisition of faults and tricks which are never corrected, and presently becomes vitia—that is to say, incurable defects of style. It is from the want of some recognised school, that beginners rush into print with manuscripts which ought never to see the light, crude, and hasty daubs, without perspective, drawing, colour, or grouping ; without, in fact, the perceptions of the elementary principles of their art.

"As soon as people have once grasped the fact—which at present they cannot understand—that fiction is a real art, an academy for the purpose of teaching it would produce almost immediate results. The effect on novelists themselves it is more difficult to estimate. First of all, it is certain that they would take more pains ; they would learn that what is easily written is hard to be read ; they would consider their situations and their characters ; they would try to give epigram and point to their dialogue ; they would realize the meaning of style which, to some who write novels, seems at present a word absolutely without meaning ; in a word, they would acquire the first principles of their art and endeavour by every means in their power to be correct. At first, then, the novels published would be fewer in number, and there would be even some destruction of apparently established reputations. Meanwhile all the clever young people would be attending lectures, taking lessons in style, practising the arts of description, dialogue, and character drawing, devising plots, and learning the great secret of Selection. Thus, after a while, the same thing would happen, as is now happening with painting, the market would be flooded with novels, much more correct in form and expression than those which now flutter their little unregarded life of a moment; there would be fewer sins of commission and omission, fewer absurdities, fewer vulgarities, less slip-shod writing, in fact, an extraordinary improvement."

This admits my whole contention in writing this book, viz., that literary Technics are quite as essential to the writer as originality or genius, especially bearing in mind, the ever intensifying competition in all the fields of Literature.

# IV.—THE DRAMA.

*The Drama, the earliest of literary forms, its ancient phases " Property," pieces—How to acquire Dramatic Technics—A promising outlook—Schlegel's advice to young writers for the Stage.*

IT must have struck many thoughtful minds as singular that the Drama—the most ancient form of concrete Literature—if the expression may be employed—should be comparatively so much neglected as it is by contemporary writers in our own country. The origin of the Drama was doubtless due to the love of imitation inherent in man, and the wish to put himself in the place of others. The Old Testament abounds in the dramatic spirit, and a true dramatic poetry existed at an early period among the ancient Hindoos.

Greece was the true birth-place of the genius of the Drama in all its varied phases, and Greece, too, has furnished to the world the only plays which do not pale their ineffectual fires even in the sunburst of Shakespeare's genius. Tragedy, including all the modern phases of sentimental or poetic dramatic action, and comedy, running down to farce, were alike the invention of classic Greece, and how large a measure of the splendid intellectual energy, creative power and intense passion of that remarkable people, found its proper expression in a true dramatic form!  A whole Literature was, indeed, created, and a resultant philosophy, so that the Greek national Stage came to be chief among the political and social factors in the development of the people at large.

It seems strange that the young literary aspirants of our own day should in general, seek for anything rather than exposition on the Stage.  Much has been said, and eloquently too, on the decay of contemporary dramatic Literature, and on the growing evil of what may be justly termed purely mechanical, or " Property " plays. The reason is not far to seek.  Few young writers of promise turn to the stage as a probable outlet for their intellectual activity.  They believe that Managers do not want originality, that they are insensible to the highest literary beauties, that the strains of pure and passionate poetry, and the richest conceptions of imagination are not wanted there; that in a word Carpenters, Engineers, Chemists, Costumiers, and dancing masters are alone in command of the situation, and that the drama must be abandoned as a purely intellectual pursuit.  This is a fallacy, however, and a little reflection and observation will prove it to be so.  That Managers do not readily " believe " in offered MS. plays is true enough, but that is due to the low average merit of the pieces sent in. If we soberly examine the absolute merits of successful acting plays of the present day, we shall certainly find them quite inferior, with but few exceptions, to the best novels, or other imaginative works of the day and an evidence is shown here in the fact that very successful novels are usually dramatized.

It may be depended on that what will constitute a commanding success in the form of an imaginative work, should if cast in a dramatic mould, be much more successful, when invested with the overpowering realism of the actor and the scene.

One great obstacle, no doubt, in the path of many young writers of promise is the fact that they are entirely ignorant of the technics of the Stage.

They produce perhaps a piece of merit, but it is seen at once by the Stage Manager that the *sequence* of the "Scenes" alone is quite impracticable to represent.

There are many, many instances of this, and experienced dramatic readers noticing these structural defects, at once reject the piece, but almost always without mentioning the real reason, which they consider, and, perhaps, rightly enough, the author would probably not understand.

Stage technics, however, may be acquired rather easily by anyone who will take the trouble to think out the matter mechanically, especially after an inspection of the region behind the scenes which is by no means so inaccessible, by daylight, as is commonly supposed.

The structure of the theatre in its acting portions may be ascertained, too, from books, and the young dramatist should above all study *acting* plays, and that quite apart from their dialogue or plot, but solely in respect to the *mise-en-scene*, and " *Stage Directions* " generally.

Plays should be seen, too, and for the purposes of a true technical investigation, the observer should acquire the invaluable habit of taking nothing as a matter of course, but of looking for the reason why, of each *mechanical* detail of the acting.

Then, and then only, will it be seen clearly why

from an intellectual view-point, a poor play *acts*, while a really splendid piece sometimes will not, and is only fit for reading.

Then again, the young dramatist should not only study the best type of plays of all nations and periods, not even despising the drama of China and Japan, but he should carefully study, too, the great masters of Dramatic Criticism, thinkers—like William Hazlitt and Augustus William Schlegel. The Dramatic Literature of the latter is a masterpiece, and the translation by Mr. John Black in Bohn's series, should be perfectly familiar to everyone who ventures on producing any dramatic work. This book, indeed, covers in a sense the whole dramatic ground from the earliest period and includes a series of most acute and instructive observations on every species of dramatic composition. The drama is thoroughly analyzed as it existed in Greece, and Rome, while the modern Stage is exhaustively treated in Italy, France, Spain, and England.

In no single book, perhaps, may so much be learned and that in a delightful way, as from Schlegel's masterpiece, his Dramatic Criticism.

It is a library of the subject, and abounds in food for fresh thought, and for the production of new ideas.

The criticisms are always remarkable for the breadth and for the intense compression of their thought.

Volumes are packed into some of the chapters, and nowhere is there anything like diffuseness. The short monograph given of *Romeo and Juliet* is probably one of the most perfect things in this kind of Literature.

" It was reserved," for Shakespeare, says Schlegel, " to join in one ideal picture purity of heart with warmth of imagination ; sweetness and dignity of manners with passionate intensity of feeling. Under his handling it has become a glorious song of praise on that inexpressible feeling which ennobles the soul and gives to it its highest sublimity, and which elevates even the senses into soul, while at the same time it is a melancholy elegy on its inherent and imparted frailty; it is at once the apotheosis and the obsequies of Love. . . . All that is most intoxicating in the odours of a Southern Spring, all that is languishing in the song of the nightingale, or voluptuous in the first opening of the rose, all alike breathe forth from this poem. . . . The sweetest and the bitterest love and hatred, festive rejoicings and dark forebodings, tender embracings, and sepulchral horrors, the fulness of life, and self-annihilation are all here brought close to each other ; and yet these contrasts are so blended into a unity of impression, that the echo which the whole leaves behind in the mind, resembles a single but endless sigh."

The intelligent study of a book like Schlegel's is in itself a kind of dramatic education.

There is, too, another important, and highly encouraging feature to the dramatic outlook from the young writer's view-point. Theatres are multiplying, the *status* of the Actor is being rapidly elevated, and the Drama is being more and more recognised as a great factor in the National culture of the Age.

It may be fairly assumed that there is a most extensive market for really good dramatic work, and the prospects of emolument, to say nothing of the reputation or fame, to be won, are unquestionably very tempting.

The Stage is, indeed, at present the most fallow of all existing literary fields, and it waits to respond with a rich and splendid harvest if only Genius will learn how to sow the seed aright.

# V.—THE IMAGINATIVE OR CREATIVE FACULTY.

*Special Advice to Young Writers—The Continual Raising of the Standard of Literary Excellence—Sir Walter Scott and Miss Jane Porter—The Poets of the Eighteenth Century—The Imitative Faculty—Examples from Wordsworth—Young Writers and Verse-making—The Nature of Imagination—Its Application to Fiction—Fancy—What it Is—Literary Photography—Charles Dickens and his Method—The Distinction between the Literature of Knowledge and that of Power—Closing Advice.*

THE standard of average excellence in literature is continually rising, as has already been shown in this work. This is a matter much lost sight of by some young writers, for whom it has, however, a serious significance. What may be justly called the great sunburst of romantic and poetic literature began early in the present century, and it is worth remembering that even the great Sir Walter Scott himself once remarked to his friend Rogers, the author of the *Pleasures of Memory*, in reference to the rapid rise of Byron, Shelley, and others, "it is a lucky thing for us we came *before* those fellows!"

Each really good and successful work of imagination undoubtedly renders the task of the next competitor in that particular direction more arduous and complex. Thus, let us take Miss Jane Porter and her historic novels, and we can at once perceive that if published *now* for the *first* time, these works would attract comparatively but little notice, and reviewers, at best, would give them but faint praise, as feeble replicas of Scott or Lytton.

Thus, too, and especially with poetry, as the representative " general reader " grows more and more cultivated in this department of literature, he or she, naturally becomes more hard to please, and after all, literary endeavour pivots on one or both of the two great human aims or ambitions to *instruct* or to *please*.

Many, rather let us say most, of the poets so-called of the Eighteenth Century whose names, have places in biographical dictionaries and the like, would not in these days get beyond a first edition. Most writers begin, in truth, as mocking birds, and when that is the case, unfortunately they catch most perfectly the easiest notes of their favourites of the buried past, whose true greatness, however, depends on some happy, perhaps quite momentary, glimpse of " the light that never was on land or sea," as Wordsworth tells us, which is as far beyond the merely *imitative* faculty as is the moon from the infant that cries for its possession.

Let us take some examples of this. The following lines :

> *The post-boy drove with fierce career,*
> *For threatening clouds the moon had drowned,*
> *When suddenly I seemed to hear*
> *A moan, a lamentable sound,*

are taken from a ballad of Wordsworth, entitled *Alice Fell,* and in lines of about the same character as those cited, we are told how "Alice Fell" had her cloak entangled in the wheel of the "bard's" carriage, and with much metrical verbosity we are told that he gave some money to buy a new cloak for the little maid, and the poem closes with—

> *Proud creature was she the next day,*
> *The little orphan, Alice Fell !*

This, of course, is not poetry, at all, but then it is the work of him who wrote—

> *I have seen*
> *A curious child, who dwelt upon a tract*
> *Of inland ground, applying to his ear*
> *The convolutions of a smooth lipp'd shell :*
> *To which in silence hush'd his very soul*
> *Listen'd intently—and his countenance soon*
> *Brighten'd with joy ; for murmurings from within*
> *Were heard, sonorous cadences ! whereby,*
> *To his belief, the monitor expressed*
> *Mysterious union with its native sea.*

This is poetry absolute and pure, and is not to be reproduced by the mere copyist, but when we *add* to the above the two concluding lines—

> *Even such a shell the universe itself*
> *Is to the ear of Faith,*

we are overwhelmed by the sublimity of the thought, and recognise that in pure poetry alone, there resides a *seeing* spirit—a true inspiration which only of all human intellectual endowments approximates to the Inspiration which gave Humanity the Bible.

Let the young writer, in his or her early days, imitate, by all means, the work of the best standard authors, but let this imitation be always recognised as being to future production what scales and exercises are to the coming performances of the skilful pianist. The great, common, and sometimes fatal error, is for the young literary aspirant to mistake imitative for original work and, as already hinted, by comparing the *best* efforts of this kind with the *worst* published pieces of some

> *Of the grand old masters,*
> *The bards sublime,*

imagine that authorship has been actually achieved, and that fame and its attendants consequences, must be very near indeed.

It is unfortunate that poetry offers such scope for this common fallacy, owing to the fact that of nearly all standard authors in poetic literature a vast amount of absolute rubbish is preserved. This, indeed, in the face of the vast increase of literature, is most regrettable, and it were well, indeed, if we could have all our great poets thoroughly revised and divested of all useless verbosity and of all those stammerings that contrast so painfully in the ears of the cultured, with the full unfaltering notes of their truest songs, with the deep and far-resounding thoughts that *can* only issue from that really indescribable condition of mind, body, and soul, which is known as the *afflatus* of the true poet.

The best corrective, no doubt, to the evil results that usually ensue from the full indulgence given by most young writers to the imitative stage in the development of what may be emphatically called the *literary mind* is ever to be found in the careful and conscientious culture of the Imagination.

In a work of this kind it would be out of place, and useless too, to touch on the various interpretations or explanations of Imagination which perplex the world of metaphysicians. Imagination, as used here, is a term related to POETRY and the fine arts, and not only to poetry alone, but to its rival, and ofttimes its twin sister FICTION.

Let us descend for a moment to consider the facts of this entity of the human mind, which had its fullest and greatest expression in Shakespeare in profane, and probably in Saint John in sacred literature.

In the first place, Imagination deals with the real, the individual and the concrete, and is thus opposed to all abstractions or generalities which are the matters of science. Thus the imagination of an island would include local colouring of some kind, sea, shore, sky, horizon, vegetation, and so forth, whereas the scientific idea would follow the thin skeleton lines of the technical definition—a piece of land entirely surrounded by water.

With imagination is, of course, closely allied the faculty known as CONCEPTION, which is simply the power that enables us to *realise* or mentally draw a picture of what we hear or read, and the richness and accuracy of the *colouring* of this mental drawing will depend entirely on the power of the imagination, and the scope of the conception accompanying it.

Imagination, however, and this is a matter of the greatest moment to the young worker in general literature, is not simply a kind of mental photographic power. It is conjoined with a faculty for *constructive modification*, in other words, it is associated with the *creative faculty*. An artist may have little of this, and then, of his work, in words he will be a kind of photographer or reporter only. Thus, some historians are literal, matter of fact, chroniclers, entirely devoid of true insight or intuition.

The higher functions of the true and well proportioned imagination are to combine anew and add to the mere technical reproductions of persons, places, and things, those subtle strokes of happy invention and touches of new construction, which demonstrate the presence of those perceptions which are now known as the *æsthetic*. The outcome may be most various, ranging in imaginative Literature from Tragedy to Farce, but the formative faculties producing the results are essentially similar, and thus explain to us the closeness of the connection between the smile and tear, between pathos and burlesque, the sublime and the ridiculous.

FANCY, which is sometimes confused with imagination itself, is really that faculty in a state of comparative or even absolute license, together with a strange subtle mysterious creative faculty, which will work only when entirely untrammelled by fixed rules or acknowledged canons.

Fancy properly is a corruption of the Greek *fantasia*, and while in the exercise of imagination, we must always keep tolerably near nature, in fancy we may push extravagance to any degree, and make a fairy land of our own. *Ivanhoe* is a work of fine constructive imagination, but Mr. Anstey's *Vice Versâ* is a piece of the wildest fancy, and is entirely *without* the true limits of artistic imagination.

In the same way a fine bust of Plato is a work of the imagination *in excelsis*, but one of Pluto would strictly be a work of fancy.

Charles Dickens possessed both faculties in a most extraordinary degree. It is well known that in his most eccentric characters he concentrated the rich sources of his personal observation, and thus, with very rare exceptions, none of his characters were, by any means, *copies*.

This is a matter which young writers of quick observation, and having the gift of language much developed, cannot ponder too carefully. How much good and careful work has come under the notice of every editor and publisher's reader which was as far from being original, although not referrable to *any book*, as any oleograph or plaster replica of a famous piece of sculpture !

Such work may, perhaps, attain a temporary success, but it *will not live*. The writer who simply aims at photographing and reporting the world of sights and sounds in which we all move, had better turn to journalism, where he may distinguish himself greatly, and where too, he *must* be useful, but let him abandon literature in its highest and *enduring* departments.

For the mere copyists, however, there is good and useful work to do, and work that is often richly rewarded, but the first thing he should decide on is never to copy from *printed literature*. Let him go always to the originals, men, women, places, and things, the world of still life as well as that of the great human drama, and if he does this honestly and fearlessly, and determines that from his pen there shall come no second-hand work, who knows but that even for him too, shall dawn some happy season, the glorious day of that imagination, which *is* " the vision and the faculty divine."

And now a brief word as to the great distinction not always sufficiently understood between the Literature of

*Knowledge* and that of *Power.* No better or more lucid "authority" can be quoted on this head than De Quincey, who, in his remarkably terse style, observes: "There is first, the Literature of *Knowledge,* and, secondly, the Literature of Power. The function of the first is to *teach,* and the function of the second is to *move.* The very highest work," he goes on to say, "that has ever existed in the Literature of Knowledge is but a provisional work, a book upon trial and sufferance. . . . For instance, the *Principia* of Sir Isaac Newton was a book militant on earth from the first . . . as soon as a La Place builds higher upon the foundation laid by this book, effectually he throws it out of the sunshine into decay and darkness . . . now, on the contrary, the *Iliad,* the *Prometheus of Æschylus,* the *Othello,* or *King Lear,* the *Hamlet,* or *Macbeth,* and the *Paradise Lost,* are no militant, but triumphant powers as long as the languages exists in which they speak or can be taught to speak."

Surely, we have here a flood of light let in to aid us in discriminating aright between what is permanent, and what is necessarily transitory, in contemporary Literature. Knowledge, in point of fact, is always—so to speak—in a state of flux, whereas Wisdom is absolute solidarity. Thus, how little of the *science* of the Ancients remains intact, but how much of their ethical teaching is fresh and forcible, as when first formulated! To quote further from De Quincey, he adds: "The Literature of Knowledge builds only ground nests, that are swept away by floods . . . but the Literature of Power builds in aerial altitudes of temples, sacred from violation."

No one has a greater rational respect for *facts* than the writer of this book, but, in the true and lofty culture of the human mind, the *emotions* must have their part. We, doubtless, owe much to our *Knowledge*-Literature, but how much more do we owe to the impassioned Literature of Power? In this, indeed, lies the clue to the sceptical and Agnostic spirit of the day. The contemporary mind is too often overwhelmed, like Tarpeia, with the interminable riches of Knowledge and the ethical soul, alive with the emotional spirit in us all, lie deadened beneath the weight of mere matter of fact. There is, however, a true irony in the only *absolute* fact, *viz.*, that there is for the scientific man no finality in fact as discovery supersedes discovery; whereas, directly we turn to the poetic side of human thought, we *do* find much finality, and thus from an ethical view-point one *intuition* of the *true* poet outweighs in real worth to the race, in regard to infinite futurity, all the laboured conclusions of the scientist which endure only until some greater scientist proves them to be altogether erroneous.

# VI.—HOW TO PREPARE MS.

*Practical Hints—Legible Writing a Great Advantage—The
Sizes of Books—Remarks on Titles—Arrangement with a
Publisher—Rates of Remuneration—Difficulties in the Way
—Earnings of Eminent Writers.*

WE have now dealt roughly but sufficiently for the
practical purposes of this Manual, with the principal forms of book Literature, and having rapidly sketched
the nature of Poetry, the Novel, the Drama, and laid
down some broad general rules for the guidance of the
young writer, we may assume that a work is contemplated and we would now give some advice in the
humble but by no means unimportant matter of how
to produce the mechanical part of the work to the best
advantage, and to take it to market. First of all, then,
the preparation of MS. or "Copy" as Printers would
call it, is a detail worthy of some little thought by
at least the "new writer" or the young author. Nearly
everybody knows now, that one side only of the paper
must be written on, and obviously it is well that the
sheets should be of uniform size. Lined paper and,
if possible, small octavo size can be recommended, but
many writers prefer foolscap. Let the young writer
sedulously avoid all eccentricity or affectation in the prepar-

ation of his " copy." The more nearly he approaches to the character of a legal, or, let us say, a mercantile docu‐ ment the better. Genius may be eccentric, but then even genius is the worse for the eccentricity and much of the initial difficulty which we hear of in connection with the early struggles of really gifted writers, is often due solely to oddity, affectation, carelessness, and eccentricity in petty details. The great Paley produced an awful MS., and as a matter of fact, some writings of his, which may be of great value, remain to this day locked up in the impene‐ trable secrecy of an utterly illegible hand writing. Bal‐ zac wrote miserably and generally polished up crude work in proof—a most reprehensible practice. Victor Hugo converted his MS. to a mass of erasures, inter-line‐ ations and intricately traced out corrections and—great genius as he was—furnished an example to be most care‐ fully avoided, of a writer who did much work on paper that ought to be done mentally. The late Dean Stanley was another miserable writer, and at one time, in all the large establishment of his printer, there were only *two* compositors who could imperfectly " set up " from his " copy."

Let MSS., wherever possible, be kept *flat*. Never roll them up. The young and unknown writer who sends a rolled up MS. to an Editor or Publisher, may rest assured that the very first impression he will create will be one of ex‐ treme irritation. Poe, the American poet, that weird and erratic genius, used to write on interminable rolls about four inches wide, and much of his early work was proba‐ bly flung into the waste paper basket from this cause alone. It makes a busy practical man " mad," as our American friends would say, to have a mass of curling

F

papers slipping about on his desk. No one can read a MS., that has just been unrolled, in comfort, and this fact alone should put an end to what is a foolish form of folding.

Let the young writer remember that, however powerful or pathetic his literary performance may really be, however evident its beauties, those with whom its acceptance or rejection rests, will regard it solely from the business view-point of matter of fact, practical men.

Other things being fairly equal, that writer's work *must* have the best chance whose details are characterised by neatness and business-like method. To send in a really legible, properly punctuated and paragraphed MS., is unquestionably to prejudice whoever reads it in the writer's favour.

Use if possible white paper, and leave a good space between every line, and it is well to leave a margin also.

Let each chapter or section of the composition be attached by some form of paper fastener and let folios or pages of the copy be consecutively numbered.

Any words to be put into *italics* must have *one* line drawn beneath; *two* lines signify small capitals and *three* lines large capitals.

As a rule, both italics and capitals should be sparingly used. Charles Reade was very fond of typographical effects and the *Cloister and the Hearth* and *Hard Cash*, probably his two best works, contain many instances of this. Yet even here this trick, for trick it is, has added nothing to the true vividness of his wonderful style, and it is a pity he indulged in an eccentricity which is often imitated by inferior writers in a highly ludicrous manner.

There are, sometimes, cases in which it is necessary that

the MS. should be reproduced *verbatim* and *literatim*.
This is obvious in the reproduction of archaic matter and
in giving provincial dialect, and the like. When this is so,
the MS. should be distinctly marked " follow copy," and
the Printer informed of the matter, otherwise the writer
will probably have the mortification of finding his composition altered and brought into conformity with what the
compositor and Printer's Reader between them, imagine to
be correct.

It may be well, too, for the young writer to remember
that when the pages composing a work have been so
placed as to fall into their proper sequence on the sheet of
paper on which they are printed, an iron frame known as
a "chase" is placed round each group and called a forme.
The pages on the two sides of the paper are known respectively as the inner and outer "formes," every two
pages 1, 4, 5, 8, 9, 12, 13, 16, being the outer, and pages
2, 3, 6, 7, 10, 11, 14, 15, being the inner formes of a sheet
of 8vo.

Pieces of wood or metal are put between the pages to
regulate the margins of the pages, and if these are unequal, the "furniture" as it is technically called, is wrong.

The disposition of the pages so that they shall fall into
their respective places is called the " Imposition," and if in
correcting matter in page proofs the author make such
changes as draw in or drive out a page, the entire forme
.has to be re-imposed and this is a tedious and expensive
operation. Corrections should be made in " slip."

"Leads " is a name given to metal spaces placed between the lines to increase or diminish the distance between
them. This word needs explanation to some, as certain
writers of late have taken to using the technical terms of

the Printing Office, in ordinary articles and talk of " leaded matter " and the like.    The type called Pica is the standard, and the thickness of leads is formed upon this base. The thinnest lead in common use is the 8-to-Pica.    This means that eight of these would be equal to one Pica letter M in depth.

The width of the pages of a work is known as the measure, these are usually made up to Pica letter M's. The width of a double foolscap 16mo. page would be from 16 to 17 M's.

What are known to Printers as "signatures" refer to the letter or figure at the bottom of the first page of each section of a book.    This is the binder's guide who binds up the sheets alphabetically or numerically as the case may be.    The Printer's alphabet consists for this purpose of only 22 letters, A, J, U, and X, V, being left out.    The first sheet usually begins with B, leaving A for the Title, &c., which is always printed last of all.

As to types, those in general use in English are Pica, Small Pica, Long Primer, Bourgeois, Brevier, Minion, Nonpareil and Pearl.    The Pica is the largest, the others gradually diminish in size in the order in which they are given here.

Most of the news paragraphs in newspapers are in Brevier and the Market Reports are generally set up in Nonpareil, while the leaders are in Long Primer or Bourgeois.

An important part of the MS. is, of course, the title.    A book might easily be written by a curious inversion, on the title-page, and it is generally allowed that in face of the enormous mass of works issuing from the Press, the choice of a title is extremely difficult.    No better rule, perhaps, can be laid down in general than that the title should simply and correctly state what the book is, but, of course, in fiction the case is different. Even here, directness and simplicity may be commended rather than straining after exclamatory and sensational effect, which often prejudices the reader at the outset.

Reflection will thoroughly prove that in the vast majority of cases, famous books make famous titles. How few comparatively, of the greatest novels and romances of the world have titles, *per se*, in any way extraordinary. Look at *Jane Eyre, Ivanhoe, Waverley, Pendennis, Harold,* and a host of others. In truth, the title is of less importance than is commonly supposed, and no really good book can ever suffer because the title is, abstractly taken, tame or even commonplace.

The various sizes of books is a subject of some prominence in a work professing to be a guide to authorship. They vary according to the size of paper used in book printing. It may, however, be remarked that a sheet of paper folded once constitutes a folio, giving 4 pages ; this twice folded forms a quarto of 8 pages ; the sheet folded *thrice* yields an octavo of 16 pages, and a sheet folded 4 times becomes a 16mo., and yields 32 pages. In truth, these technical details are rather out of the author's province, and concern chiefly the publisher and printer, as does also the choice of paper, and of type itself. The same may be said of binding and illustrating, except in cases where the author is rich, and publishes at his own cost, in which case he may indulge his fancy and taste to a practically unlimited extent.

It does, however, often concern the author practically to know how much his MS. is likely to make in print. This is easily done if only the MS. be on uniformly sized paper, and is written pretty evenly. By counting the words hap-hazard in a few pages the average number will be obtained, and then in like manner by counting the words in a printed page of some book of a corresponding character, a wonderfully close approximation can always be obtained.

As to business arrangements with publishers, many works extant profess to lay down sundry rules and principles ; but, in truth, these are like the six and eight-penny books on law, and never apply properly to one's own very particular case.

It is, of course, understood here that the reader, who is to profit by these " Technics," is fairly familiar with the common canons of good composition, and is capable of describing, in well chosen words, things of both the thought and the fact world.

To the young author a knowledge of shorthand is of great importance, if it be not almost essential to the journalist in his noviciate. Pitman's Phonography is one of the best systems.

In the second part of this Manual will be found a full and most accurate and matter of fact account of working journalism, *per se*, but in this place we have simply to deal with the circumstance that a vast number of writers, some possessing undoubted ability, are desirous of commencing a purely literary career through the medium of some journal or magazine, although they have not the slightest idea of becoming in any sense a journalist. How journalists may become authors will be sufficiently indicated in Part II. relative to Journalism.

Let us then to illustrate what is here meant, take the

promising and hopeful case of a young writer who, we will suppose, *has* acquired as much knowledge of the true technics of literature as is possible without actual personal experience, and whose "copy" no longer exhibits crudities, and is, in point of fact, really fit for publication.

Well, then, here is a marketable literary commodity, and one possibly of real intrinsic merit.

How shall the writer dispose of it?

Why, send it, of course, to some newspaper or magazine editor.

Very well. Let us consider, there are now published in these islands two thousand and fifteen newspapers and one thousand two hundred and sixty magazines, making in all three thousand two hundred and seventy-five mediums for contemporary thought, reflection, observation and imagination, that have somehow found expression in a literary shape. There may be a few more or less, for journalistic births and deaths are frequent, but how can the ordinary unknown writer ascertain of himself, or it may be of herself, to which of these three thousand channels leading to typographical converse with the public, the precious MS. should be sent?

Ah, you reply, numbers are misleading here, the MS. is sure to be suited only to a fraction of the figures cited, and a little consideration will soon indicate the right quarter in which to send.

Will it, indeed?

Grant that the three thousand channels be certainly narrowed in the particular case to three or even *one* hundred. Well, it ordinarily occupies from one week to three weeks before an outsider can possibly obtain an editorial response to his application, and receive back his treasure marked "unsuited," or "declined with thanks."

That is supposing stamps are sent, and thus an essay on a subject of present interest and intrinsic value, would possibly make this painful round of its potential publishers, if the MS. bore this wear and tear, in from two to four or five years !

This is not the exaggeration that some may suppose. A writer, who for many years has supported himself and family, and does so now, solely on the proceeds of his literary labour, sent, in his early days, to numberless magazines, very good "copy," and never *once* had his matter accepted until after *two* whole years of sickening and heart-breaking disappointment.

The channels, however, in these days, for each kind of literary production are multiplying fast. First, keen competition increases the number of more or less parallel publications ; and, secondly, more and more journals and serials are becoming very catholic, indeed, in their selection of matter.

The main idea underlying most editorial work now is, less what is strictly suitable than what is popular, and thus papers related to grave and serious subjects, now admit in many cases matter of a very miscellaneous character, provided only it be entertaining or emphatically readable.

Books, so to speak, of all kinds, are being rapidly broken down for serial purposes, and thus it has come about that there is positively no single class or kind of literature, that is unrepresented in the newspaper or periodical press.

This is so far, of course, greatly to the advantage of the young writer, especially to those who have acquired the invaluable art of perspicuous and effective compression. But obviously, the difficulty of making the right application with "suitable" copy in the right quarter increases with the facility thus given.

The fortunate producer of really good "copy" on almost any subject in these days, embodying new ideas, thoughts, or fresh information, not in the way of ordinary readers, may be *sure* that there is *somewhere* a channel for his particular production, but such knowledge, although certain as anything inferential can possibly be, is aggravated by the circumstance that it is practically impossible to take advantage of the fact, and thus the opportunity for an appearance in print is lost, while futile endeavours are made in quarters where, if the writer only knew the circumstances existing, the MS. would never become an unwelcome guest.

Obviously to meet such cases as these—and how numerous they are, the very fact of this Manual coming into existence shows conclusively—some elaborate organization was needed which should do for the embryo writer what he cannot possibly do for himself, viz., take selections of his best work, and having ascertained their real fitness for certain literary openings, waiting here and there to be filled, straightway harmonize supply and demand, and convey his copy exactly where it would be available, and thus, as far as practicable, eliminate from the initial— *i.e.*, the heart-breaking disappointing period of every literary career—all the uncertainty and suspense, and put the young writer to a crucial trial of his or her true powers without their being wasted and worn, in a more or less vain struggle for a success rendered nearly impossible under the usual conditions that environ nearly all literary beginners.

To some of our readers it will, therefore, be indeed welcome news to be assured that such an organization as that indicated above, does exist, and that it is in full force under the name of The London Literary Society, especially designed to take up the good work of young writers, and bring that work into the precise quarters where it will be really welcome, and that with a directness and certainty, beyond the power of any individual.

By the establishment of this Society the very thing is actually accomplished, of which the late Lord Lytton drew an ideal in one of his novels, and this result is gained, that no writer of merit can fail of success, who avails himself of an association which, sooner or later, must of necessity find the right market for every kind of good literary work entrusted to its care.

Such a Society is the nearest approach to that ideal Guild of authors imagined by the late Lord Lytton, and has, indeed, real advantages over such a Guild, could one be established, which are as evident as they are practical. It furnishes in itself the only possible solution to the problem—so often set by cruel circumstances to the young writer in his early days—and wherever the Society is utilised, and it is open to all—it becomes certain, not only that no work, great or small, of true merit can be lost to the world, but it becomes certain, too, that the author shall not be left without a reward at least adequate to the ability, or it may be, the genius, of which that work is the visible expression.

And now let us pass to that interesting subject, literary remuneration.

Much has been written on the subject of the pecuniary gains of celebrated writers.

Nearly every book dealing with the literary life has something on this head, and usually more or less incorrectly.

It is an interesting, but hardly a practical subject, and yet we may well suppose that every writer is, more or less, stimulated at times by a remembrance of the splendid prize that Literature does sometimes bestow on her favourites.

It is certain that in this country the Golden Age of great authors did not begin much before the present century.

A few poets like Pope and Dryden, received somewhat considerable sums for the age in which they lived, but Walter Scott first showed that a large fortune could be earned by the pen, making in all over £110,000. For *Woodstock*, by no means his best story, the author of *Waverley* received £8,000, and for *Childe Harold*, Lord Byron received £600 for each Canto, receiving in all for his poems about £23,000.

Thomas Moore had for *Lalla Rhook* £3,000 paid in advance. Lord Beaconsfield made £10,000 by *Lothair*, which is very far from being a great novel, but was enhanced by special political reasons. His lordship is said to have cleared over £30,000 by Literature.

*Romola* realised £7,000.

Charles Dickens received for *Our Mutual Friend* £24,000, a very great sum indeed for a single work, and several living novelists like Wilkie Collins, can now command very large sums in advance for their novels.

The late Lord Lytton made by his novels £80,000 ; and Anthony Trollope realised, in 20 years, full £70,000.

The great continental writers have also been remarkable for their success, in a pecuniary point of view.

Lamartine had for his History £20,000, and £1,800 for *La Chute D'un Ange.*

Victor Hugo received for *Notre Dame* only 2,800 francs, but his subsequent "price" for a complete work was fabulous.

Thiers sold his famous History for £20,000, and Chateaubriand made about £22,000 by his principal works.

Strangely enough, and constituting a great fact-Satire on the age—of all living authors, probably, M. Emile Zola makes by his pen the largest amount, his ordinary income being calculated, in 1884, at no less than £12,000 a-year.

# VII.—FICTION AS AN ART.

*A New Idea—Reference to Painting and Sculpture—Crude Realities—Victor Hugo—Some Examples.*

IT has been well said that language is to the writer what pigments are to the painter. One is an artist in colours, the other should be in words. I say *should be* intentionally and deliberately, because it is obvious that whereas the painter in covering his canvas must follow out some sort of rule, and be obedient to general canons of proportion, of shade, of light and of general harmony, the writer, that is the worker in words, often acts as though he were a law to himself, as though exceptions formed rules, and as though outrages on every just idea of proportion, and even propriety, constituted the certain sign of the most advanced literary genius.

Eccentricity, or worse even, is sometimes substituted for method, and we have discords in sentences, phrases, and paragraphs, which, if perpetrated on canvas or uttered in music, would be unanimously scouted as altogether barbarous and utterly intolerable.

In ordinary writing, articles of all kinds, news reports and general descriptive matter, rules exist which are not greatly violated, for the simple reason that editors will not pass anything of the outrageous character, but far differ-

ent is it with Fiction, notwithstanding that Fiction has been
rightly called an art, and is universally allowed to be a
very high form of art indeed.

The striking and richly suggestive question has been
raised of late, and is referred to in a previous chapter:
can we teach fiction as we teach painting or sculpture?
Of course, in one sense, no art can be literally taught, unless,
indeed, the pupil possesses the true art receptivity,
and the true art impulse, but art is still governed by laws
of its own, like those of harmony, and, essentially, it
matters nothing whatever whether that harmony finds
expression in colours, sounds as in musical notes, or in
articulate words.

In painting, for example, everybody knows in these
days what is meant by *technique*, and that most decidedly
can be taught very clearly. It were vain to expect that
everybody could be taught how to tell a story, just as it
were vain to expect that everybody could be trained so as
to paint in oil or carve in stone. But surely it will be
readily granted that, given in the individual a real faculty
for narration, it is obvious that this, *plus* the true *technique*
of story-telling, must be immensely more effective, than
the faculty left, as it often is, to grow disproportioned into
a thousand eccentric shapes, and, finally run to waste,
through the absence of system or discipline.

Taking an extreme case of a man of transcendant
original genius, Victor Hugo himself was a paradox, for
he was one of the best and the worst story tellers who
ever took up a pen, and often, he inclined distinctly to
be the worst. His narratives are frequently, as in many
episodes of *Les Miserables*, about the most inartistic things
that can well be conceived, and never does he show any-

thing like the consummate art to be found in many contemporary sensational novelists who do not collectively
possess a tithe of his wonderful genius.

Why should we not have a school or an academy of
fiction ? For one thing, it would effectually stop the publication of the miserably defective essays in story telling,
which we so frequently meet with now, and which are
redeemed only by some secondary merits which probably
have nothing to do really with fiction at all. A picture
entirely out of perspective, full of wrong lights and shades,
and generally a series of brush blunders, could not get
hung, and surely if the art of Fiction were reduced to a
system, certain books, which are outrages to the name of
Fiction, would never see the light of publication.

Criticism would be greatly relieved, as it would be at
once clear whether or not a given work of Fiction was
conformable to, or in utter violation of the known canons
of artistic story-telling.

Novelists naturally would benefit, as they would be
shamed out of slovenly work and taught that the genius of
the true Story Teller is not merely a question of photographing or reporting.

Much in real life that is reproduced in Fiction does not
belong to Fiction as an art at all. Were it not thus,
every daily Journal almost would be a cluster of incipient
novels.

The crude notion of some writers of Fiction so called,
seems to be that anything and everything may be verbally
reproduced and that the more faithfully this is done, the
greater is the success achieved ! This is art with a ven-
geance indeed.

Take the case of two novels that lately came before the

writer. The one was the work of an experienced author, and although the story was "thin" and by no means original, the narrative was well proportioned in its various episodes, the conversation or dialogues, although by no means brilliant, were skilfully done and the general effect was somewhat artistic, although the work was one of little absolute merit. The writer, however, had been trained and disciplined, knew the canons of good taste and obeyed them, and consequently produced a book which if it did not greatly please, did not in any way irritate one's critical faculty.

The other work was evidently by a writer possessing a considerable gift of language, an exuberant imagination, and some invention. But there had been no restraining or guiding faculty at work, and the book might furnish passages to illustrate nearly all the worst faults of composition of this kind. In the one case there was not much colour, but it was skilfully disposed on a small canvas and made a *genre* picture which did not offend. In the other instance masses of strong colours were daubed on a vast canvas, without regard to harmony of composition, and the general effect to the trained critical faculty was simply hideous. This need not be; surely it were practicable to do for Fiction what has long since been done for painting. Mudie is of much more recreative moment to the nation than the Royal Academy, and the general culture in right canons of art of all our young incipient Novelists would certainly be a national gain of no inconsiderable magnitude.

Finally, we would remark that, as a local answer, at least, to the oft-asked question—What are the most *popular* Novels?—the subjoined statistics, furnished by the chief librarian of the Birmingham Free Libraries, show that the following is the order of Birmingham's favourite twenty novels. The figures denote the number of times that the several books were issued from the Central Lending Library : *The Pickwick Papers*, 389 ; *Bleak House*, 361 ; *David Copperfield*, 303 ; *Robinson Crusoe*, 294; *Oliver Twist*, 278 ; *Martin Chuzzlewit*, 224 ; *The Mill on the Floss*, 217 ; *The Arabian Nights*, 211 ; *Ivanhoe*, 200; *Vanity Fair*, 195 ; Mrs. Wood's *East Lynne*, 188; *Adam Bede*, 181 ; Mrs. Wood's *Channings*, 143 ; Kingsley's *Westward Ho!* 139 ; *My Novel*, 137 ; *John Inglesant*, 134 ; *The Vicar of Wakefield*, 133 ; *Middlemarch*, 129 ; *It's Never Too Late to Mend*, 121 ; and Miss Worboise's *Father Fabian*, 119. The only book in other departments than fiction, which would be entitled to a place on the above list is Tennyson's Poems, 135.

# VIII.—ON THE CHOICE OF BOOKS.

VERY obviously a Manual professing as this does to supply the young and necessarily inexperienced writer with all the information that *can* be vicariously imparted, would be very imperfect, indeed, if it did not take into full and very careful consideration the very important and even vital matter of what should be read, the more especially as with regard to certain forms of Literary work, this takes the significant shape of what *must* be read, unless, indeed, the young writer wilfully places himself at an extreme disadvantage with all his competitors.

In the previous sections, great stress has been laid on the avoidance by young writers of all copyist works, so far as books are concerned, and this in truth cannot be too much insisted on, but, then *per contra*, in order to write books that will be heeded by others, many books need to be read, *pari passu*, if possible with the continual and intelligent study of persons, places, and things. Reading, we are told, on high authority, makes a full man, and in days like these of universal intellectual activity, reading, at all events, on the part of the literary worker, should be extensive and yet highly eclectic and having laid in as permanent mental capital, a large stock of the Literature of the Past, it is essential that a fairly exhaustive acquaintance be maintained with the salient forms of contemporary Literature.

What shall I read—and still more, what *must* I read—are becoming in these days difficult questions to answer in a perfectly satisfactory manner, but one thing is certain, that every writer who works in general Literature should make a point of becoming thoroughly familiar with all kinds of what may be more conveniently called epochal Literature. Under this head come, necessarily, writers like Virgil, Horace, Petrarch, Dante and Milton, and many who, although infinitely inferior in point of actual genius still mark turning points or distinct episodes in the Literature of their respective countries and periods. Another important point is this. There are numerous books that include in each a virtual library so that by reading, not skimming one of them, a perfectly practical knowledge can be obtained thence of a great number of other works, ignorance of which, cannot fail to be a loss and may be a peril to the inexperienced writer.

Human life is not long enough and human circumstances, even were life extended to double its usual span, do not permit that any person should ever approximate to reading even all the great books of the world, but it is quite within the power of the ordinary literary student to master fully all the *epochal* books in each of the principal departments of permanent literature. Thus Paley's Natural Theology, with his famous argument of design, is epochal, and so too, in Poetry was Scott's *Lay of the Last Minstrel* which indirectly led to the Byronic legend of the Corsair, the *Bride of Abydos* and subsequently a multitude of metrical romances which for a long period imparted an entirely new character to English Poetic Literature.

Most writers, however, are ready enough to read Poetry and History, story and romance, but there too many stop. In days like these science must be remembered even by the writer who proposes to revel exclusively in the fairy realms of a creative imagination. Fact, properly disposed, lends oftentimes an indescribable charm to Fancy, and in such a conspicuous instance as that of M. Jules Verne we may see the amazing success wherewith a most industrious writer has laid the whole world of science under unceasing contribution and has produced thence some of the most fascinating tales for the young, ay, and the old too, that have probably been written in any language. All kinds of fact-knowledge are more or less valuable to the writer in general Literature and of facts, indeed, there cannot well be too many. But, of course, to profit fully thence, not only must the assimilative faculty be carefully trained, but the reproductive faculty too. One important piece of advice remains. There are few persons, and these will hardly be found among young writers, who do not now and then come across some word, or allusion, or expression in their general reading which they do not properly understand. Unfortunately many readers, especially the young, pass on, and are content to remain ignorant of what they deem a trifling matter. A golden rule for the reader who would fully profit by reading is never to do anything of the kind, but immediately to refer to the dictionary, or other book of references or to ask some one who may be supposed to know, or if these things cannot be done, to carefully mark the place and clear away all ignorance of the matter at the earliest opportunity. Anyone who does this honestly and faithfully for a few years so as to constitute it a fixed habit, will by that means alone amass an amazing amount of really practical knowledge that otherwise would have been permanently lost to them.

# IX.—ON THE CONSTRUCTING OF PLOTS.

I T will be remembered in a former chapter devoted to an historical and general consideration of the Novel as a work of literary art, a passage from a leading article in the *Times* was cited as confirmatory of the position taken up by the writer of this Manual that there is a system of literary technics, if only we can apply them properly, as surely as there is a grammar to the language. Every painter in oils, whatever may be his ideal, has to reduce his most beautiful conceptions to a rough sketch, to a mere black and white outline, and has, so to speak, to map his way along although the final exit may be a rainbow blaze of dazzling beauty, an Aurora Borealis of heavenly hues. That many writers have been eminently careless constructors of stories, that some, like Sir Walter Scott himself, have started tales without the least idea how they were to end, are no reasons why the young writer should trust to invention where method would serve far better, or leave to the chance of a fortunate intuition, what might be certainly supplied by the simple organisation of Industry. Visit any extensive collection of paintings and how much bad drawing, how many false " lights," how great a number of impossible foreshortenings, to say nothing of other solecisms, will be visible to the skilled critic, and all of these are solely due to ignorance, more or less wilful, to carelessness, idleness, perversity or some infirmity that militates against the artist producing that which is the great end of Art—a perfect thing. Observe, something perfect, not necessarily great or sublime, but complete and self-contained, faultless within its own limit and serving as a type and a standard for succeeding endeavours in the same direction.

One of the main objects of this Manual, as will be readily perceived, is to inculcate above all things the unspeakable importance of taking pains, of attending minutely to detail, of investing every piece of literary work with the utmost finish that it is susceptible of receiving, and generally of avoiding all forms of careless, slovenly, or, in any sense imperfect work.

Genius, of course, of an absolute character, will surely work out its own way and no set of cut and dried rules will greatly avail in cases where the writer either from having much or little ability, is self-sufficient. It may make some smile to hear of a writer having too much ability, but judged from a purely artistic view point, Victor Hugo spoiled one of his greatest prose works simply from overloading it—often at the most ill selected places, with an excess of digression, of interlude, of historic reference, and generally an extraordinary wealth of superfluous material.

The writer who would avoid an error injurious to genius and entirely fatal to mediocrity or even to considerable talent, should study *classic* as well as romantic novels. Walter Savage Landor, for example, is the very antithesis of Victor Hugo. Every historic allusion that does occur in the writings of the great author of the Imaginary Conversations goes straight to the mark, the finish of each detail only so far as that detail fills an appointed and necessary place in the symmetrical perfection of the whole. Victor Hugo, however, on the contrary, is continually lavishing the richest gifts of a splendid creative fancy where they are more or less futile, except to amaze one with the mental wealth and the reckless waste of that wealth by the writer.

Again, a glance over the vast fields of literary history will serve to show how certain and enduring is the reward always won by work whereof the finish is very great, if not perfect, and it is quite certain that all very highly wrought work is bound to live.

Just as the painter, after choosing the subject and determining on the general lines of its treatment, must prepare a sketch, is it best for the writer to map out as it were the general course of the narrative and plot composing the particular novel to be written. The plot indeed, is the mainspring, the pivot, the prime motor and ought to be, at all events, true to two things—itself and human nature and its environments—the circumstance of Life. It is assumed that the young writer is at all events somewhat acquainted with the elements of Euclid and even the examination by anyone previously unacquainted with geometry, of any of the propositions of Euclid will show at once how great is the beauty of any piece of pure intellectuality which leaves, so to speak, no residuum, but is absolutely complete in itself and rounded off on all sides to a perfect finality.

William Godwin, the famous author of what has been called the earliest form of the sensational novel in England, *Caleb Williams,* was specially careful in the construction and elaboration of his plot. That of the work in question

was completed in advance of the story and worked back-
ward, and, other things being equal, this kind of mathe-
matically perfect story must always fascinate the great
majority of readers, and it furnishes above all other kinds,
the species of interest which *holds* readers and forces them
to read on to the end.   There are novels and novels.
Some, in point of fact, are destitute of plot, and very many
indeed remind us of the well worn lines of Cowper who
even in *his* remote day complained that ;

> " Novels, witness every month's review,
>    Belie their names and offer nothing new."

But we are speaking here only of good and careful
work, the only kind of writing worth anybody's while in
these days and it will ever be found that when the con-
structional lines are clearly, cleverly and intelligently laid
down, the writer will discover that the verbal part of the
task will be better in proportion, very much as the flowering creeper is ever displayed to the greatest advantage on
a symmetrical trellis, than when it is left to lose half its
loveliness and all its symmetrical proportions, through being
abandoned to a state of luxurious tangle and universal
confusion.

A little practice, however, is worth much precept, and
probably until the writer has made some bad plots
—supposing the bias be towards Fiction, very good ones
can hardly be expected.   There can be no question but
that the shortest and safest road to success in this department of what we may call fine art literature lies in the
honest and careful study of really good models.   In general,
neither Scott nor Dickens were ever good at plots, and it
may be said that as a broad rule, the plot, is, perhaps, of

minor moment when the whole of the writing is delightful
and abounds in incident and really good character delineation. Still, unless the young writer erects a high standard
of ideal excellence, what is actually done will hardly be up
to the mark, and writers, whose special power lies in the
natural evolution of a complex plot to a simple logical and
inevitable explication, cannot be read too carefully. Mr.
Wilkie Collins and the late Lord Lytton are both conspicuous for the thoroughly workmanlike character of their
plots, and these, indeed, have, as all such work of the
best quality, should, the spontaneity of a natural growth.
Let the young writer above all things, avoid as far as
possible the use of that fatal *Deus ex Machinâ* which
always irritates the veteran novel reader and the veteran
reviewer too, and let the development of each phase of a
plot be strictly cumulative. This is the method of the
greatest master of the art although expressed in dramas
which are after all, our stage novels and romances, and a
close acquaintance with Shakespeare is most decidedly an
essential part of the necessary mental training to which
the writer should submit, if a fair working knowledge
of the hidden laws of the art of plot-making on a
really good basis is to be gained, before bad habits are
formed and, perhaps, confirmed by a success gained
by excellence in things besides the plot itself.

## X.—LITERATURE FOR CHILDREN.

CERTAINLY if the age is more exacting than the good old easy-going times, in respect to the young writer —if more is asked year by year from the producer of books in all departments of Letters—a very ample compensation is found in the much greater variety, and far more expansive character of the many fields of Literature now open to every young author. One special department, for example, that of children's books, may here be cited as an illustration of the richness and promise that exists for young writers who deliberately lay themselves out to write for the young.

Two striking instances naturally suggest themselves at once of really splendid fields opened by two writers, very differently endowed from each other, by the way, and now serving to indicate that further worlds of infinite profit and pleasure may be created yet for the millions of young readers of the immediate future. Jules Verne, in his *Fairy Tales of Science*, and Lewis Carrol, in his fantastic, grotesque, outrageous, but exquisite fooling, have each exhibited entirely new and, until thus revealed, unguessed phases of Literature of this class, and what may not yet be done to amuse or instruct the children of the future?

It has been aptly said, by a well informed writer on this subject, that books were not expressly written for children much before the day of Perrault and Madame d'Aulnay. If there were children's books earlier than these, it would require a clever bibliographer to name them. Children were either left to their own devices, or kept extremely hard at work, and flogged with earnestness. We hear in the record of the youth of many famous men and women, Lady Jane Grey, Montaigne, Agrippa d'Aubigné, and others, that they could read Greek, and Latin, and Hebrew at an age when modern children are not out of the nursery, but surely boys and girls who were so precocious, and were birched and beaten so unmercifully, cannot have had time to study children's books, even if such treasures had been within their reach.

The present, however, is an infinitely happier age for young folks of all classes, and it is universally understood that they are to be amused and instructed, generally by one and the same means, and a common consent has authoritatively decided that one of the most popular agencies for effecting this consummation is simply a Literature invoked especially for the boys and girls of the period, from babyhood to youth. Books, above all things, are the best recognised and most popular forms of presents for children, and when we reflect a little, what vast opportunities are here disclosed for the writer who shall deliberately train the literary faculty within, to provide exactly what is suited to the true needs of the contemporary child! There is a rich mine of literary wealth to be worked out here, and the material lies all around in the greatest abundance.

# XI.—THE ART OF READING.

*A Writer's Bibliography: Chronology, History, Renaissance Literature, French, German, Italian, Dutch, Danish, Swedish, Russian, Swiss, and Spanish Literature—Suggestions for Acquiring Special Forms of Literary Knowledge—Pouring out and pouring in—Reading Rapidly—Appropriating and assimilating—Importance of facts to the Novelist—The late Lord Lytton—How to ensure success.*

HAVING sketched in outline, in a previous chapter, the general tenour of what should be the reading of the young author, it will be well to append, as briefly as possible, a short bibliography, so to speak, of works that should be at hand when required. Very few, comparatively speaking, can, of course, reasonably be expected to possess a tithe of the works here catalogued, and it is also obvious that many of them will be but rarely needed in even rather comprehensive literary work, but each of the list will be found on occasion indispensable, and as these works can always be consulted in the large public library, or at all events in the reading room of the British Museum, a *resumé* of some of the best books in most departments of human knowledge that are valuable for consultation purposes will be useful as a guide to many.

In Chronology, then,—and dates are all-important in

a variety of magazine, as well as book-work—Sir H. Nicholas's *Chronology of History*, Blair's *Chronological Tables,* W. Hales' *New Analysis of Chronology*, and L. Sage's famous *Historical Atlas* may be recommended.   •

In Geography, there are Bunbury's *History of Ancient Geography*, E. A. Freeman's *Historical Geography of Europe*, Louis Kappen's *World in the Middle Ages*, and Murray's *Ancient Atlas.*   •

In regard to Ancient History, we have Dr. J. Priestley's *Lectures on History*, Bolingbroke's Letters on the study of the same, Bossuet's *Discourses*, Keightley's *Outlines*, and Sir John Stoddart's *Introduction to Universal History.*

It has been already stated that Dictionaries are necessary, and it is only needful to add here that Hadyn's *Dates*, Smith's *Bible and Classical Dictionaries*, and Woodward and Cates' *Encyclopædia* are admirable works.

A good general idea of Ancient Law may be obtained from H. S. Maine's exhaustive work on *Village Communities*, &c.

In Oriental History—a subject now brought into greater prominence daily in relation to our Indian Empire—Max Duncker, Baron Bunsen, Sir G. Cornwall Lewis, Professor Rawlinson, Niebuhr, Baldwin (*Prehistoric Nations*), and De Coulanges on *Ayrian Civilization*, are all standard works.

Babylon, Chaldea, and Assyria are severally dealt with by Layard, George Smith, A. H. Sayce (*The Empires of the East*), and Hackness.

Egypt can be read up in its ancient aspects in the pages of Wilkinson and Sharpe.

For Bible History, the student should consult Dean Milman (*History of the Jews*), Dean Stanley, Sir Edward Strachey, Ewald Caum Cooke (*Origins of Religion and*

*Language*), and Kenrick, whose *Phœnicia* is an excellent work.

Greece and Greek History must not be overlooked. We have Mitford, unfortunately tedious, but, *per contrà,* full of sound, good matter, Grote, Thirlwall, Cox (*The Athenian Empire*), and Ranke.

These should be supplemented by Mahaffy's *History of Classical Greek Literature*, Gladstone's *Juventus Mundi,* and Freeman's splendid *Essays*.

Rome and the Romans naturally involve more extensive research. Gibbon's *Decline and Fall* is, of course, indispensable. Added to this, are Arnold (*History of Rome*), Keightley, Merivale, Dyer (*The Kings of Rome*), F. W. Newman (*Regal Rome*), *Plutarch,* by George Long, and Forsyth's *Life of Cicero.* These works ought to be supplemented by Sismondi, Guizot (*Civilization in Europe*), Smythe, Thierry *Histoire d'Attila*), and W. C. Perry's *Franks.*

The Middle Ages will detain us longer. The principal writers who *must* be mastered by any writer who desires to deal with the period authoritatively, are certainly Hallam, Michelet (*History of France*), Meuzel (*History of Germany*), Machiavelli (*History of Florence*), De Comines (*History of Louis XI.*), Froissart and Monstrelet, Coxe (*History of the Crusade*), Freeman again, Ralston (*Russia*), and some others, which will be suggested to the student, in many instances, by the above.

The Renaissance period ought to be mastered generally, and to accomplish this it will be necessary to consult the following writers :—J. A. Symonds (*History of the Renaissance in Italy*), Roscoe (*Life of Lorenzo de Médici, and Leo X.*), Washington Irving, Froude, Helps (*The Spanish Conquest of America*), Mitchell's *Life of Wallenstein*, Prescott, Ranke, Motley (especially *The Rise of the Dutch Republic*), Sully, Cardinal Retz, Macaulay (remembering that he is an extremely partizan writer), Hume, and Lingard.

Later periods, coming down to our own times, will be found fully treated by Voltaire, St. Simon, Pepys, Evelyn, Burnett, Clarendon, Bancroft, Carlyle (*Oliver Cromwell*), Coxe (*House of Austria*), Crowe, Yonge (*History of the Bourbons*), and Burke.

The great French Revolution has a Literature of its own. The indispensable authorities are, Thiers, Sir Walter Scott (*Life of Napoleon*), Taine, Lecky, and Carlyle. Finally, in English, there is J. R. Green's truly admirable *History of the English People*.

This, though much, is very far from all that a general writer should read, or be prepared to read, on occasion.

Science has its own special historians, and among the chief of these are the Duke of Argyll, Sir D. Brewster, Professor Huxley, D. Lardner (chiefly for popular purposes), Mary Somerville, Professor Tyndall, William Whewell, Sir W. Thompson, Graham Bell, De Morgan, Richard A. Proctor, J. W. Dawson, Hugh Miller, Dr. Carpenter, Sir Charles Bell, and very many others.

Philology is a study of great importance. Words are the materials in which the writer works, they are his stuffs and tissues, his pigments and tones or notes, and he cannot have too accurate a knowledge of the language at all events in which he writes. Young writers should acquaint themselves well with the philological labours of Horne Tooke (*Diversions of Purley*), Max Muller, Isaac Taylor (*On the Alphabet*), and J. M. Kemble (*Anglo Saxon*).

In Political Economy, there are the works of Fawcett,

Jevons, J. Mill (carefully avoiding his miserable scepticism), J. R. McCulloch, Ricardo (*Rent*), and N. W. Senior.

In Moral Philosophy it is necessary to study Sir W. Hamilton, McCost, Hegel, Kant, A. Bain, Herbert Spencer (avoiding all his irreligious tendencies), J. D. Morell, and Mansel.

Something should be known fundamentally of British Jurisprudence, and for this Blackstone is a good and convenient manual.

The Fine Arts ought to be cultivated, through the medium of books, as well as by actual observation. To do this, the works of Ruskin and Professor Colvin will be found of the greatest use.

In Theology, it is well to read Archbishop Whately, Trench, (especially on Miracles and Parables), Tait, Dr. Julius Hare, Charles Kingsley, Keble, Pusey, H. J. Irons (who has admirable matter set in a bad style), E. H. Plumptre, and some others whose names will naturally suggest themselves.

Poets and novelists need not be particularized here. Inclination, coupled with the necessary leisure, will usually lead the young writer far enough in these naturally attractive directions.

In French Science, we have, in Chemistry, Thénard, Gay, Lussac, and others ; In Astronomy, there is Arago ; in Zoology, G. S. St. Hilaire ; Natural History, Desmarets ; Botany, Jussieu, the illustrious rival of Linnæus ; Electricity, Ampère ; and in Heat, Séguin.

In Philosophy, we find Joubert, Pascal (by all means master and fully assimilate his noble " thoughts "), Victor Cousin, and Quinet.

In Political Economy, there are Bastiat, Chevalier de Tocqueville, and Say.

In Sociology, there are Lacordaire, Père Hyacinth, and St. Simon.

Political Literature is strongly represented by Chateaubriand, Madame de Stael, Lamartine, Montalembert, Louis Veuillot, and Bishop Dupauloup.

Among Historians, are Louis Blanc, Michelet, Bourrienne, and Barbaroux. Others, like Thierry, have been already mentioned.

In Poetry, we have Victor Hugo, Béranger, J. de Chénier, Casimir Delavigne, Ponsard, Gautier, and Lamartine.

Literature in general has been dealt with by Saint Beuve, G. Sand, Jun., Balzac, Buloz, Merimée, Jules Verne, and Madame de Genlis.

In Fiction, we must not forget Alexandre Dumas, De Vigny, Erckmann-Chatrian, and the realistic Zola.

German Literature is such a vast, almost shoreless ocean, and has such unfathomable depths, that it is impracticable to do much more for the average English writer than indicate the manner in which he may most profitably skim the surface.

In Science generally, we have A. V. Humboldt, Oken, Helmholtz, H. Müller, and Dopler; In Astronomy, there are Encke and Biela; in Chemistry, Liebig and Whöler; in Botany, Sacks and Moldenhauer; in Physiology, Von Baer and Voihow; and in Materialist Philosophy, there is the godless Haeckle, for whose baseless atheistic conclusions a capital antidote exists in the justly famous Boston Monday Evening Lectures of the eloquent Dr. Joseph Cooke.

Germans have dealt with Ancient Classic Literature in

H

an effective and sometimes singularly humorous manner. In this department will be found the following:— J. G. H. Hermann, F. A. Wolf, K. O. Müller, Dindorf, and Bekker.

In Philology, we must not overlook Bunsen, Schlegel, Bopp, and Grimm.

In Poetry, there are Bürger, Claudius, Fouqué, Heine (whose sneering profanity stains what might have been a really great genius), Körner, Count Stolberg, Tieck, Werner, Uhland, Kotzebue, Schiller, and Goethe.

In German Philosophy, a knowledge, more or less complete, is desirable of Herder, Fichte, Schelling, Hegel, Schopenhauer (the exponent of Pessimism, who contends that the human will resists—as it certainly does—reason and right), and Hartmann (the founder of the Philosophy of the Unconscious), are the chief stars.

Italian Literature should be glanced at. In History, we find Lombardi, Count Troya, Farini, Rossi, and P. Verrari ; in Politics (always a special subject of the acute Italian mind), Giacomo Leopardi (a poet, by the way, and a particularly unhappy one), Mazzini, and Lanza ; in General Literature, Ugo Foscolo, Silvio Pellico, and Niccolini; as poets, pure and simple, there are, besides the grand old bards, Dante, Petrarch, Farini, Giusti, Rossetti, Caetani, and a few more.

Dutch Literature need not detain us long. Jacob Von Lennep is a poet and novelist well worth reading ; and so, too, is H. Conscience, on account of his excellent novels.

In Danish, acquaintance should be made with Oersted, and, of course, with Hans Andersen.

Sweden has for Science, Berzelius ; for History, Otto ; for Poetry, Tegner ; and as a novelist, Miss Bremer.

Some general knowledge should be sought of Russian Literature. This may be obtained by recourse to the works of Poushkin and Lermantoff (poetry); Gogol (tales of Slavonic life); Turguenieff (who influenced greatly the emancipation of the Serfs); and, as a supplement, one reading of Sir John Bowring's capital Anthologies will give a very good general idea of the distinctive features and mode of thought employed in Hungarian, Bohemian, Servian, Polish, and Russian poetry.

There is a compact modern Swiss Literature. Vinet, for Theology; Agassiz, De Saussure, Pestalozzi, and Zimmerman merit mention. The careful student will not fail to make acquaintance with the works of Lavater. A careful study of the drawings, and of the rules laid down in his remarkable work on Physiognomy cannot fail to be of real service to the writer of Fiction.

Finally, reaching Spain, we may enumerate Cervantes, Calderon (the Iberian Shakespeare, in the estimation of some), Quevedo, Gareid, Toreno, and Moratin (who has been called, and I believe very justly, the "Spanish Molière").

Many careful readers will find omissions in my lists, but my object rather is to be suggestive than exhaustive. Recourse to the writers named will generally result in more or less acquaintance with kindred authors, and thus the student will be led on insensibly to a more and more advanced form of culture. And here we would just say one word to those—especially the young, and those who may not have read very extensively—who may feel at first some dismay at the prospect of work here opened before their eyes.

Obviously, no arbitrary rules can or should be laid down,

but ready means are merely suggested here for acquiring particular forms of Literary knowledge as occasion may require. It is no uncommon thing for the young writer, having been set some particular work, to go round asking, " What must I read ? "

As to the general mass of reading involved, it is surprising how rapidity and accuracy can be made to go together by any student who once resolves to thoroughly master every work he takes up. It has been said that Dr. Johnson used to tear the heart of every book, and the phrase is by no' means far-fetched. Practice in reading, as in other matters, makes perfect. Let the writer remember that he who proposes to pour out matter from his pen point fit to engross the fair attention of men and women, should not fail to take in very much matter too, and render his reading and writing reciprocal. Even to the novelist, a very wide knowledge of facts is of essential value. There is positively no department of human knowledge that is not occasionally laid under inquisition by the writer of Fiction, and much, very much, that to the unreflecting reader may seem such smooth and easy writing, is oftentimes the outcome of really hard study and research. Thoughtful readers, for example, of many of the late Lord Lytton's novels know well how copiously he drew from books of all kinds, and yet with such a consummate skill that very much indeed of what he appropriated he made his own in an absolute sense ; rather, indeed, what he *assimilated*, for in this lies the whole art and mystery of successful reading for literary reproduction. Read, then, to assimilate, and to the writer who does this, and lets the thoughts and ideas of others be as seed in his mind, to fruitify later on, full literary success at last is a foregone conclusion.

# XII.—COPYRIGHT.

COPYRIGHT, although so important to authors, is properly understood by but few. The Act regulating Literary Copyright generally, is Victoria 5 and 6, c. 45.

The following are the salient and essential features :—

1.—Copyright in any book published during the writer's life, lasts during the remainder of that life, and for seven years beyond it, but with this very curious limitation, viz., that no copyright can endure beyond forty-two years. This clause is, therefore, a little contradictory, but we must suppose that the framers imagined when they decided to limit the duration of Copyright, that no author could survive his first book so long as forty-two years !

2.—If a book be pirated the remedy lies in an ordinary action at law.

3.—Touching the right of re-publishing articles of all kinds, or stories in periodicals, books of reference, and the like, the author must, previously to the publication of such matter, formally reserve his right. When this is not done, the copyright is vested in the editor for twenty-eight years. After that period it lapses to the author.

4.—In point of Law, copyright is personal property.

5.—In order, however, to secure copyright in any work, it must be registered at Stationers' Hall, where a Register is kept for that purpose. The fee is only five shillings.

The officers at Stationers' Hall, Stationers' Hall Court, Ludgate Hill, will afford any information that may be required on the subject.

6.—Of every new book or new edition, five copies must be sent to the following Libraries:—That of the British Museum; the Bodleian, Oxford; the Public Library, Cambridge; that of the Faculty of Advocates, Edinburgh; and Trinity College, Dublin. A penalty is incurred for omission of the value of the book and five pounds beyond.

7.—To secure a copyright in France for works published in England, Registration must be effected at the Bureau de la Librairie of the Ministry of the Interior at Paris. The cost is under seven francs.

8.—Copyright Conventions now exist with Prussia, Saxony, Saxe-Weimar, Saxe-Meiningen, Brunswick, and some other German States.

It is in place to record here, that, at the close of 1885, the following account was published in this country, as the Results of the Berne Conference on Copyright. It appears that after much debate, the Convention adopted a *definitive* scheme for an " International Union " for guarding the rights of literary, musical, dramatic, and artistic property, which now only awaits the sanction of the countries represented, and the adherence of any other countries who might like to join it. France, Germany, England, Italy, Spain, Belgium, Holland, Sweden, Norway, Switzerland, the United States, the Argentine Republic, Hayti, Honduras, Paraguay, and Tunis were officially represented. The Conference determined to give to the literature and art of all countries adhering to the union complete protection in each country during the existence of the copyright in the country of origin, or in the country in which a copyright is invaded, whichever is the shorter period. Also, to give an author the exclusive right to translate, or authorize a translation of, his work for ten years, instead of for one year, as provided by most international treaties. Also, to treat a translation as an original work. Also, to give the author of a work of fiction the exclusive right to dramatize it, subject to the internal copyright laws of the country of origin of the work, and the country of the appearance of the dramatized plot. The Minister of the United States was not authorized to take any part in the discussions, but he laid before the Convention an official assurance that his country accepted the principal that all literature should receive the same protection, whether produced by its own subjects or the subjects of other nations; adding that, although the question was surrounded by difficulties, they ought to yield to some international general arrangement which should be equitable and simple.

As I write on this very important subject, an animated discussion is in progress, not only in Great Britain, but on the Continent, and especially in the United States of America, on the way in which a really permanent and perfectly equitable International Copyright Law can be established, so as to extend its protective influence to *all* members of the great Republic of Letters.

Every one knows the feud long existing between authors and publishers on the two sides of the Atlantic, and the way in which British authors have suffered through the piracy of American publishers is but too notorious. It has been certainly alleged that England has retaliated, although this does not in the least affect the true merits of the case, but we believe if the details were thoroughly sifted it would be found that English publishers have in general behaved towards Transatlantic authors in a very different spirit from that commonly evinced by American towards English writers. In illustration of this, some one having started the question, how much did Longfellow obtain for his English editions? Messrs. George Routledge and Sons recently made public the following facts as to the sums of money they have paid the representative American poet or his representatives :—*New England Tragedies,* £1000 ; *Translation of Dante,* £500 ; *Tales of a Wayside Inn,* £250 ; *In the Harbour,* £200 : *Aftermath,* £200 ; *The Divine Tragedy,* £150 ; *The Masque of Pandora,* £100 ; *Kéramos,* £60 ; *The Hanging of the Crane,* £50 ; *Flower de Luce,* £18. Where, one naturally asks, can a like instance be adduced of an American firm of publishers really reciprocating this generous action—for generous it is, remembering the absence of any International Copyright?

That something legislative should result out of the Parliament of 1886 is only what might be justly anticipated when we consider how well and strongly the literary element is represented in this particular House of Commons. There are in all about forty men of letters, including Mr. Justin McCarthy, the well-known author of *Serapion*, and Mr. G. O. Trevelyan, who wrote the racy *Ladies in Parliament*, giving a vivid poetic picture of a Female Legislature, wherein occurs the capital passage in which the Lady Matilda, bewailing the difference between Palmerstonian and Gladstonian M.P.'s, remarks :—

"Sucking Statesmen seldom failed in seeing
    The final cause and import of their being ;
    They dressed, they drove a drag, nor sought to shirk
    Their portion of the matrimonial work ;

They flocked to rout and drum by tens and twelves,
Danced every dance, and left their cards themselves."

The later Liberal is thus described :—

" By travel taught less sharply to recoil
  From notions grown on Transatlantic soil ;
  Weaned from the creed of all his Kin and Kith ;
  On Bentham nursed, and fed on Goldwin Smith ;
  His one supreme intent, through woe and weal,
  To hold by Gladstone as *he* held by Peel.
  In social wiles unversed, a rumoured ball
  Extracts from him no mild suggestive call ;
  Nor deigns he in the ranged quadrille to stand,
  Unless to claim a fair constituent's hand,
  Or serve some party end."

Then there are Mr. Thorold Rogers, translator of the *Bacchus of Euripides*, Mr. Beresford Hope, Mr. John Morley, Mr. A. J. Balfour, author of the *Defence of Philosophical Doubt*, Sir John Lubbock, Sir Lyon Playfair, and others who have long since made their literary mark in the age.

# APPENDIX.

FOR the young versifier I would strongly advise a careful study of Pope's *Essay on Criticism*, the title of which is a little misleading, as this fine essay in and on metre refers specially to the metrical essay of the young and inexperienced. Then ordinary English metres can be looked up in the "Prosody" section of most English Grammars, or in the Encyclopædia, while some note should be taken of the principal classic metres, of the *Cæsura*, or division, viz., the separation of verses into two portions, consequent on the ending of a word in the centre, and other like matters.

In English verse, the prevailing feet are the Trochee and the Iambus, with the Anapæst occasionally worked in. These have been dwelt on in section 2, but some further observations on metre rhythm, the sonnets, and *vers de société*, and burlesque are needed here to round off this part of our subject.

A line or verse may, within reason and breath, of course, consist of various number of feet, and these need not be alike, but a certain harmony must always be maintained, and words obviously difficult to enunciate musically, should be carefully avoided. For this, Byron's earlier poems—his tales, for instance—are good models, as their verbal music is often very marked indeed, as in such passages as the following :

> " A single Rose is shedding there
>     Its lonely lustre, meek and pale,
> It looks as planted by Despair,
>     So white, so faint, the slightest gale
> Might whirl the leaves on high,
>     And yet, tho' storms and blight assail,
> And hands more rude than Wintry sky
>     May wring it from the stem—in vain—
> To-morrow sees it bloom again ! "
>
> \*      \*      \*      \*      \*
>
> " To it the livelong night there sings,
>     A bird unseen, but not remote ;
> Invisible his airy wings,
> But soft as harp that Houri strings,
>     His long entrancing note !
>     It were the Bulbul, but his throat,
>         Tho' mournful, pours not such a strain ;
> For they who listen cannot leave
> The spot, but linger there and grieve
>     As if they loved in vain ! "

Very simple and ordinary are the words here marshalled together with such metrical skill, but what an effect is produced, both sound and sense harmonizing at the mournful close, and ending with a sigh, not expressed, but *felt*.

Byron was equally happy with the decasyllabic verse, the favourite measure of Pope, and in the nine lined, or Spenserian stanza, produced some of the brightest gems of English poetry. *Childe Harold* abounds with fine examples.

For narrative and general purposes of description and philosophizing, the six lined stanza, *i.e.*, a quatrain with a closing clinching couplet, is extremely flexible and adaptable, producing excellent effect when skilfully employed. The late Lord Lytton used it in his noble epic, *King Arthur*, a poem far too little known. The following may be taken as an illustration of the way in which this six lined stanza may be made to resemble the sonnet in its accumulative and self-contained completeness :

> " How often joys most true are least intense,
>     For simple pleasures last the longest hour !
> This is the happiness of Innocence :
>     Where is the magic like the gladdening power
>         That findeth peace in Life's most common grass,
>         Nor lets a single blade untasted pass ? "

Or this, on Spiritual Loveliness :

> " There is a Beauty that appealeth to
>     The spirit, more than to the earthly sense,
> Like harmonies that world-wise Plato drew
>     From the starr'd heavens : 'tis the charm intense
>         That lives in Beauty of that rarer kind,
>         That makes the flesh the mirror of the mind ! "

The "to" ending of the first line of the last stanza is faulty, however, but the subjoined shows how good metrical *sound*-effects may be produced in a yet more simple form of verse :

> " By Night I stray in some moonlit way,
>     To bathe in her clear, cold light,
> On the lakes I float, in a silver boat,
>     And am woo'd by the water sprite.

I ascend the stair of some star beam rare,
And far from the earth I climb,
Till with ravished soul I hear the roll
Of the mighty spheric chime ! "

The subject here is the all-prevailing Spirit of Poetry.

Regarding blank verse, the first known specimen in English is a translation of the second and fourth books of Virgil's *Æneid*, by the Earl of Surrey, executed in 1547. Blank, although generally confined to heroic metre, *i.e*, verse of ten syllables, or five feet, may be broken up into stanzas of lines or verses of various lengths, as in Southey's well known *Thalaba*, Longfellow's *Hiawatha*, and some of Shelley's poetry. *Dramatic* blank verse is specially distinguished by the unaccented, or superfluous syllable, allowed at the end, as in the well worn passage :

" To be, or not to be ? that is the *question :*
Whether 'tis nobler in the mind to *suffer*—"

Unfortunately some so-called metrical writers when they abandon rhyme, forget that the very greatest art and pains are essential to prevent blank verse becoming simply prose chopped into arbitrary lengths, and merely rising and falling with an intolerable monotony.

In reference to this, the author of what claims to be a practical guide to the whole art of English versification has seriously sought to prejudice English rhymed verse, and substitute therefor a miserable assonance alone, like path and way, and the like !

In burlesque, comic verse, and especially in *vers de societé*, the finish and accuracy imparted by the writer cannot be great, but, of course, the art should be cleverly concealed, and the effect appear to be natural, and no way forced.

As models for work of this kind, the writer should study the *Ingoldsby Legends*, the works in this direction of Wolcot, Thackeray, Hood, Praed, and Locker. Praed is quite a model himself of elegance, accuracy, perspicuity and point, and a couplet of his, sometimes quoted as an instance of fulness, without over doing it, runs thus:

> " She was a very pretty Nun,
>     Sad, delicate, and—five feet one ! "

Finally, touching the verbal structure of the sonnet, I would add that the best authorities decide that there are only *three* genuine sonnet forms. These are the Petrachan, the English or Shakespearean, and the Miltonic, the last having unbroken continuity. The rhymed closing couplet is, strictly speaking, only proper in this last form. Then in a really perfect sonnet,—perfect as to *form*,—the octave, or major portion, must rhyme with the same sound for the first, fourth, fifth and eighth lines, but the sestet or minor portion may be more varied. In point of fact, but few English sonnets fulfil all the strict requirements of the laws laid down for their production by those who have made the structure of the Sonnet a veritable metrical science.

# JOURNALISM.

## Part II.

# I.—INITIAL.

IN the First Part of this Manual I have endeavoured to discuss practically the principal forms of book Literature wherein the writer may engage his or her powers with the best prospects of attaining success.

Obviously, however, with an extraordinary multiplying of books, newspaper and periodic Literature has made marvellous advances and those entering the defined paths of professional journalism, may and often do, find that therein lies their best road to successful authorship.

Originally nothing of a literary character could be much farther from the book, as understood by our forefathers, than the news sheet, but that is all changed now and not a day passes but we read in journals articles which are really *disjecta membra* of veritable books that might be, and which sometimes are to be. Many a piece of merely " descriptive reporting," as it would be lightly termed by the Editor in whose sheet it appears, is found day after day which is fully up to the standard of the very best novels as far as writing goes, and many a leading article appears that if it had been penned for the *Spectator* would have become a part of English Literature.

This being so, it has been deemed well to add further to the utility of the Literary Manual as a full guide for the writer by giving a Second Part entirely devoted to a copious, but strictly practical, consideration of Journalism, and comprising in a series of brief monographs the principal points of practical interest for those who are desirous of becoming Journalists, either as their literary finality or to make Journalism their path to ultimate authorship.

With this object in view the following chapters have been composed. They embody what has been strictly the actual and personal experience of the writer and may be relied on for accuracy in every detail.

Beginning with an historic sketch of the newspaper ancient and modern, these chapters include what may be justly called practical descriptions of the whole of the duties and functions of the working Journalist. The different types of contemporary newspapers and periodicals are described, and as it is desired to enlighten writers as to the ethical sides of the profession, some observations are appended on what appear to be most certainly some defects and even blots on what is rightly held to be, as a whole, among the foremost triumphs of the nineteenth century.

# II.—THE NEWSPAPER PRESS.

### *Its Historic Aspects.*

THE earliest newspapers of which we have any certain knowledge, were the *Acta Diurna* of the ancient Romans, although the fanciful archæologist may assume, if it so pleases him, that the ancient Babylonians may possibly have published laconic periodicals in the shape of hieroglyphic bricks or slabs, on which the achievements of their men of light and leading were duly recorded.

Fancies aside, the nucleus and very germ of the newspaper proper, is undoubtedly the news-paragraph—and thence it follows that the "Reporter" is the true and original producer directly or indirectly, of all that heterogeneous mass of matter which comprises the contemporary news sheet. It is known to most persons that the earliest examples of the modern journals are German or Venetian. In the 15th century certain small news sheets entitled the *Newe Zeytung* appeared in several of the principal German cities and these were issued just in time to contain accounts of the discovery of America while the official *Notizie Scritte* issued at Venice in the 16th century, gives quite a chronicle of the many aggressive wars undertaken by that intensely aristocratic Republic. The price paid for these sheets—a small coin known as gazeta

—gave rise to the name gazette. The *English Mercury* with its report of the Spanish Armada is now proved to have been a forgery, but in 1619 Mr. Newbury published the probable parent of modern English Journalism under the odd title as it seems of *News out of Holland,* and a few years later, we find what is quaintly called *The Certaine News of the Present Week* edited by Mr. Nathaniel Butter. The civil war—inimical to the arts and Literature—was very favourable to the newspaper Press and a whole host of partisan hornet like sheets began to fly about amid the fire and fury of a fraticidal strife. The titles of many of these are curious. Thus we have *England's Memorable Accidents, The Parliament's Scout, The Scots' Dove,* a large bird, I opine, with capacious beak and sharp claws— *The Secret Owl* and the *Mercurius Acheronticus.* In none of these is there anything even remotely akin to what is understood as editing. The original matter is poor enough to us, removed at so great a distance from the times, but doubtless contemporary readers thought differently and the partisanship shown is of the most unreasonable sort. The first English newspaper, properly speaking, was established by Sir Roger L'Estrange in 1663, but it lapsed on the advent at Oxford two years later, of the famous *London Gazette,* which thus includes in its life of over two centuries the whole sequence and range of our modern Press.

When the excitement of the great Rebellion had entirely subsided, it became difficult to fill even the small space comprehended by the current journal and some Publishers inserted what they believed to be suitable passages from the Bible. How some of these old fashioned God fearing Parliamentarians and Cavaliers, would stare at one of our nineteenth century sheets, crammed full of humbug, lies, vice, violence, crime, and virtual blasphemy! However, there were others possibly equally pious, but more practically economical, who would leave blanks in which the reader was politely informed he might write his own letters before sending on the journal to his friends.

Until the reign of Queen Anne, it was quite exceptional for any journal to appear at intervals of less than a week. The Duke of Marlborough, however, changed all that, and such was the national eagerness to read of his encounters with the French, that 17 newspapers sprang up of a more or less daily character.

*The London Daily Post and General Advertiser* was begun in the year 1726 and about a quarter of a century later became the *Public Advertiser*. It was in this Journal that Junius first wrote his historic letters.

It is believed that in the year 1880 the total number of newspapers and periodicals published all over the world was 34,274 and the circulation of these was computed to be 10,592,000,000! In round numbers Europe had twenty thousand daily, weekly, and monthly papers and North America over 12,011, a very significant fact, if we consider the enormous difference in point of population between the two continents. Asia had some 700—the great bulk of these being Indian or Chinese—and Australasia had over 600—an enormous number when we reflect that the population of the whole of the great group is not very much over three millions.

Who will deny that the present is a newspaper age, or that on the general character and tone of the Press depends very greatly the political, social, and religious status of the people?

Although strictly speaking outside the scope of this work, a few remarks on the Continental Press may be acceptable to many readers. It is generally admitted that the first authentic Parisian Journal was established as long ago as the year 1631, by a physician, one Théophraste Renaudot. Cardinal Richelieu regarded the scheme with more favour than might have been expected, and a Royal Privilege was accorded to the Gazette. After running its course until 1762, this veteran Journal took a new lease of life, became a bi-weekly and for the first time combined advertisements with news.—The initial daily French newspaper was, however, the *Journal de Paris* which lived from 1777 until about 1819. The Revolution of 1848 was singularly prolific in Journals and over a hundred political organs lived and died under the rule of Napoleon III. *The Feuilleton,* that special feature of French Journalism dates from the early days of the first Napoleon when the peril of original leading articles was too great for writers to risk as a rule, and accordingly the spare space was filled with some kind of fiction. When the age of cheap newspapers set in under the auspices of Emile de Girardin, the novelist if successful, was much sought after by the French newspaper proprietor and Eugene Sue, for instance, received for his *Wandering Jew* 100,000 francs, while in later times M. Zola has obtained truly enormous prices for his sensational fiction.

Taking a hasty glance over the rest of the Continent, we find that in the low countries the Pioneer of the modern Press was a war Gazette entitled *Niewetijdinghe* which curiously enough was illustrated. This rude organ was started as long ago as 1605 and was ultimately merged in the *Gazette van Antwerpen* which died early in the present century.

Germany had no newspaper properly so called, until 1615 when Frankfort led the way with a gazette of its own. In Italy as already intimated, Venice furnished the first Journals of the peninsula, but for a long while the fulmination of the Vatican, especially the famous Bull of Gregory XIII. kept the Press down and it was only on the advent of the benign Pius IX., that Italy began to exercise the functions of political and partisan Journalism. It is noteworthy that the land whence our Street Punch originated, is rich in comic periodicals and news sheets which agree well with the genius of the mass of the people, and exercise no small influence at times on affairs of state.

As to the Iberian Peninsula during the seventeenth century, small sheets called *Relaciones* appeared at intermittent periods. These gave accounts sometimes true and sometimes false, of curious matters, and when news ran short or invention was at fault, romances were inserted— romances usually that any educated Northman would deem it a penance to merely skim over. The Peninsula War gave the first stimulus to Spanish Journalism, but such was the extraordinary license of the early newspapers of this secluded land, that in 1824 the Government suppressed all except the *Madrid Gazette* and a few sheets of a simply scientific or mercantile nature. Only imagine the state of a nation in this nineteenth century which could allow a Bureaucracy to sweep away its Press at a stroke!

The Spanish Press is in fact to this day at a very low ebb and that of Portugal is insignificant, if not contemptible.

In the Scandinavian Peninsula the first journal appears to have been the *Ordinarie Post Tidende* which lasted from 1643 till 1680, and was then succeeded—a great mark of progress it was doubtless considered—by *Rela-*

*tiones Curiosae*, a paper entirely in Latin! Then the Press took a turn and became French, but ultimately native journalism came to the front and now nearly every town in Sweden and Norway—towns which *we* should call villges in most instances—has its local organ.

The Press of Denmark is quite recent and calls for no special remark.

In Russia the newspaper, like most other marks of civilization in that country, is the creation of Peter the Great. The great autocrat superintended the Press himself and kept his Editors in order by the knout and axe. For a long time political journalism had no existence, but after the invasion by Napoleon, new latitude was given to Russian journals and one of them the *Sjëwernaja Ptsch'eta*, *i.e.*, the Northern Bee, attained to a very large circulation. The *Journal de St. Petersburg*, the organ of the court is in French and has a very important circulation outside the Empire—as to the Russian journals generally, the names of many have become familiar to us through the agency of the foreign correspondence in our own daily Press. It may be fairly said of them, that they are all under the absolute authority, often most capriciously and cruelly exercised, of an irresponsible Bureaucracy. Roughly speaking, the Muscovite newspapers are either official or Panslavic and considered in the light of ordinary European Press organs, they are impotent as a rule, although now and then they contrive to sting the Governmental censors into vengeful reprisals.

The Turkish Press is comparatively modern. The earliest Ottoman news sheet appeared in 1795 and it was only about 1825 that any real progress had been made in establishing news journals among a race singularly incapable of appreciating or supporting a national Press. The only Turkish Journal of much importance is the well known *Djeridei Havadis* which was started in 1843 by an Englishman born in Turkey. There are besides the *Terguman Ahwal, i.e.*, The Interpreter of Events and *Tas Veeri Evkiar*, The mirror of Thoughts. These and, indeed, all Turkish papers too often have no " Leaders," and properly speaking are rather news magazines than newspapers in our acceptation of the word.

As to the *Levant Herald* that is rather extraneous to, than native of, Turkey, and is in fact, a literary exotic that is ever and anon killed by a rigorous censorship only to reappear after a few months in some fresh form of hostility to the *statu quo*.

Greece is very well supplied with newspapers, there being about 80 of which the greater number are issued at Athens, thus maintaining well the gossip loving character of the ancient Athenians.

Thus much for the Press of Europe. Crossing the Atlantic, we find in America the true habitat of the typical contemporary newspaper. In the United States the Pioneer Paper was the venerable *Boston News Letter* founded in 1704 which after various vicissitudes finally died in a quixotic attempt to represent the claims of King George in opposition to those of the new born Republic.

About the time of the Revolution, the new England colonies had 14 Journals, but in 1800 there were in all 200 and in another decade these had increased to 359, of which nearly 30 were issued daily. By the year 1850 the number was 2526 and in 20 years more these had swollen into the prodigious host of no less than 5871 distinct Journals. Now the number is very much greater and these are supplemented by an army of periodicals of all kinds. It is a curious fact that few of the very best leading periodicals have in America what we should call an enormous circulation ; this arises from a variety of causes and one of these is the extraordinary subdivision of Parties in the United States and the immense number of militant interests that have to be represented.

In the Australasian colonies the Press has flourished during the last quarter of a century in a manner little less than marvellous. Every Australasian town however small, has its special organ of opinion and many have several. The great Metropolitan Journals such as the *Melbourne Argus*, the *Sydney Morning Herald*, the *Adelaide Register*, the *Brisbane Courier* and the *New Zealand Herald* are conducted exactly like our best London newspapers and contain really able articles, while the Parliamentary Reports would do no discredit to our own *Hansard*.

The development of the Australian Press is in all ways remarkable, as it is greatly in advance of the natural increase of population. I have, as I write, before me No. 98 of the *Melbourne Medley* of Saturday, August 29th, 1857. This sheet declares itself to be a " Political, Moral, Religious and Anti-political advocate." It is printed in good plain type in four small double column pages and opens with Shipping Intelligence. It then records, without any separate heading, the fact that, " Chan Sigh and Tzan Seing are now under sentence of death for the murder of Sophia Lewis." The " Editor " adds this curious note. " Murder will out. Selfishness led to the murder. Mankind might know that no murderer can be otherwise than miserable, and from the very principle of self love they ought to avoid it."

The " they " is slightly ambiguous not to say ungrammatical, but the reasoning is sound and does credit to the
Editor's Morals. The rest of the contents include a Crown
land sale, "a melancholy reflection on the number of
coroners' inquests arising through intemperance," a plea
for the Chinese, a " Lecture " about 40 lines long, a
" Warning " being a scripture quotation and a wholesome
exhortation therefrom, in fact an Editorial sermon, half-a-
dozen lines in length, and nearly a page of advertisements.
The price is stated to be one shilling and sixpence per
quarter ; and the imprint curtly runs, " Printed for R.
Service, Proprietor." From the *Melbourne Medley* to the
*Melbourne Argus*, what a marvellous transition ! It is less
than the usual estimate of ordinary human life but it
includes the development of the greatest community ever
known to human history.

# III.—THE PRINTING OFFICE.

*Early Books—Transcript Making in Ancient Rome—Etymology of " Book "—The Contemporary Printing Office Described.*

STRANGELY as it may seem to some, the Newspaper or Periodical is, after all, the great and special product of the Printing Press.

It is now about four centuries since the discovery of the method of printing from movable types, and yet before two of these centuries had elapsed, the Newspaper may fairly be said to have passed its embryonic stage.

The art of making books, however,—*i.e.*, the mechanical part only,—is far older than Rome itself. Now, although the Newspaper, as we see it, could never have been but for the modern Printing Press, Literature would in all certainty have advanced to nearly, if not quite, its present nineteenth century position, with this difference only, that it must have remained, to a great extent, the heritage of the few rather than that of the many.

No doubt these views will to some seem, at first, very extreme, but it should be remembered that the extraordinary multiplication of books at a very cheap rate, has really added little, if anything, to the solid mass of absolutely original Literature. Thousands of books, indeed, belonging to the popular type are, after all, simply slight intellectual exfoliations, as it were, from authors who would surely not have remained quite silent, even in the absence of a Printing Press.

It is curious enough that the word "book," derived from the Anglo-Saxon *boc*, is, with certain modifications of spelling, common to all the Northern tongues. Philologists generally derive the word from the same root as "beech," and the earliest works of some of the Norsemen were undoubtedly written—or rather engraved—on slips of wood from the beech tree, which thus merits an honourable place in the practical history of our more modern literature.

Everybody knows that the Greek *Biblos*,—a book,—is simply derived from the ancient Egyptian name of the Papyrus, and that the volume meant originally the strips of written papyrus rolled around the cylinder.

Perhaps, however, everybody does not know that it was no less a personage than Julius Cæsar who, in his despatches to the Roman Senate, first introduced the more convenient method of dividing the scroll into the form of the modern book. Such literary productions were known as "paginæ," and from these we derive our word "page."

Under Cæsar Augustus, the art of making books,—namely, that of multiplying copies of approved works—flourished exceedingly. Later on, during the dark ages, a few patient and pious monks might be found here and there slowly and laboriously toiling at the production of various MSS., but it was only in the palmy days of the Eternal city that the Romans appear to have manufactured books in fair quantities, producing, in many cases, what may be called respectable editions of good classics. The papyrus, we are told, was carefully prepared for the labours of the professional scribe, who effected his task with a reed pen—*calamus*. The ink—*atramentum*—was generally very good, and would put to shame much of that in use at the present day, for in some of the MSS. found among the ruins of Herculaneum, the characters yet remain quite distinct.

Suppose a Roman author wished, as we say, to go to Press; he sought out some firm of publishers, and having, in some way, arranged "terms" with them, his work went into the hands of the professional Reader, who read, or rather recited, the matter to some fifty transcribers (librarii), who corresponded to the compositors, using the pen in place of the "stick," or metal case employed for setting up the type a few lines at a time, and had to work with ears, eyes, and hands at once. Directly the transcribers had produced the number of copies required, the MSS. went to the *librarioli*, *i.e.*, artists who ornamented them with various dainty devices, and from these the rolls passed to the *bibliopegi*, or bookbinders. Finally, the works reached the *bibliopolae* (the booksellers), and were then offered to the reading public very much as in our own days. In many instances these classical productions were probably fully equal in beauty of workmanship to some of those mediæval illuminated works of which we hear so much.

The modern Printing Office is quite another thing. It generally includes some of the very best results in the development of steam power and engineers' work, and, bearing in mind the character of the products turned out, occupies a primary place of importance among our national manufactories.

London Printing Offices vary very greatly—not so much in point of size, as in their internal economy and general management. Some, indeed, decidedly reflect discredit on their proprietors, and are a blot to the localities to which they belong. The great majority, however, are well managed in these days, and especially is it so with the one here taken as a type of the contemporary Printing Office.

The building covers a very considerable area, and is divided nearly through the centre, in order to obtain additional light and air—very important matters to printers.

The basement includes a series of well-built brick chambers, devoted to the storage of very many tons of paper, and the damping of the same; while above, on the various floors, are the spacious composing rooms, each with its vistas of "frames" (the name given to the stands supporting the cases of type at which the compositors work), each picking up letter by letter, the types required to form the words on the MSS. or "copy" before him.

There is in this establishment a store department, which is in itself a most suggestive sight, by reason of the enormous quantity of material always in stock. All is properly arranged exactly as you might find the "specimens" in a good geological cabinet, and each man is served with whatever he wants in the most methodical manner. Tons and tons of type lie here, and, not to go into unmeaning figures, it may be mentioned that the type in the establishment referred to, would, if laid side by side, suffice to go round the earth at the meridian of Greenwich.

Everything here is managed on a basis of the most exact discipline. In some offices the composing rooms are scenes of the wildest uproar, and are, in general, very objectionable, consequent on the prevailing tone of the desultory gossip and broad "chaffing" that too often

characterise them.   Benjamin Franklin once pronounced
a London Printing Office to be a " sink of iniquity."   Here,
however, anything of that kind is absolutely unknown,
and a tone of decided intellectuality, and even refinement,
pervades all the departments.

The machinery section—two very long chambers containing nearly fifty of some of the finest printing machines
in the world—is a very interesting sight.   Especially is
this so when they are all at work throwing off hundreds of
thousands of various journals, magazines, or sheets of
books, and impressing one with an indescribable sense of
stupenduous force.

Everything here is on an enormous scale, as may well
be imagined.   A good notion, however, of the resources
of the firm may be obtained from a visit to the department
devoted to the storage of stereo plates.   These are kept,
for obvious reasons, in fire-proof vault.   One store house
is a large chamber some thirty feet long, devided into five
alleys, giving access to the sets of pigeon holes which
reach from floor to ceiling—some fifteen feet—each of
which contains one sheet, in stereotype or electrotype plates,
of various works which have received the distinguished
honour of being sterotyped.   When it is added that of
these pigeon holes there are reckoned to be seventy thousand, some idea may be formed of the care and thought
required to keep such a mass of matter in perfect order,
so that any set of plates wanted, may be forthcoming at a
moment's notice.

Dimly lighted with a wire guarded gas burner, these
vistas of little black cells hold, doubtless, some of the best
results—we may suppose—of human thought and imagination, and one could not remain wholly unmoved, nor forbear

from reflecting how much of life's best sunlight—of life's truest social pleasures, and of home's best and purest joys must, in many instances, have been sacrificed in order to obtain the dubious fame of an inch or two in the stereo stores of a great printer!

Many of the plates had never seen printers' ink, and probably never would! Even shrewd publishers now and then make mistakes, and seriously misunderstand the public taste; and thus the author, who has, at last, reached what is rightly held to be the crowning honour of being stereotyped, may, and sometimes does, get no further than the cells of the printer's electro stores, and after being in the books of the storekeeper for a certain period as a mere number and initial, will finally be melted down to give place to the work of a more successful rival. *Sic transit gloria mundi!* Subsidiary to this, there is a department where corrections are made in stereo plates, generally the result of the author's afterthought; and then, again, there is an important section of the establishment devoted to the safe keeping of blocks—the books of reference, containing the proof impressions, forming quite an interesting series of art albums.

The motive power to drive the array of printing machines is supplied by three fine boilers and as many engines, and all these are kept in the best order; indeed, they resemble, in their smartness, the locomotives of passenger trains, and offer a very remarkable contrast to the engines of some establishments, where the driver's *habitat* closely approximates to something between a pigstye and a dustbin. Then, too, whereas in many offices the "readers," or correctors of the press, are obliged to perform their very difficult and responsible duties in any

K

awkwardly placed hole or corner, here each has a private room,—small, but convenient, well lighted and ventilated, and provided with a good desk, shelves, and pigeon-holes. The reader thus has his little library of reference at hand, and fulfils his functions under the most favorable conditions possible.

Some seven or eight hundred persons are employed in various ways in this establishment, which is decidedly a model for all printing offices ; and the completeness of the organization throughout is only equalled by the evident solicitude of the principals for the physical and moral well-being of all their employés, from the least to the greatest. This marked solicitude is practically expressed in various ways :—There is a library containing some hundreds of useful and entertaining books ; a good school has been provided for the boys ; and the general arrangements for the associative benefit of the employés include cricket and athletic clubs ; an institute, to which was attached an excellent magazine, serving as a useful medium of intercourse between the various members of the whole large body, and a valuable record of all that in any way affects the common interest ; together with some admirable economic provisions. Among these, is a savings' account, in which the men may place whatever sum per week they think fit, until a total of £100 is reached, and on which five per cent. interest is paid. There is also a savings' bank for boys, in which they may place small sums, until a total of £1 is reached. The inducement offered to the boys to foster saving habits is a rate of interest, of which the half would gladden the hearts of thousands, if they could get it.

The firm has also for some years past set aside a portion of the profits, which they have divided amongst those who have earned £70 and upwards, in the proportion of their earnings. The amount is credited to each man in the savings' account. It must remain in this account three months before it can be drawn out, interest being paid on it in the meantime, This division, however, can only be made while the business yields a fairly adequate return, and the firm is careful each year not to pledge themselves to make it in any subsequent year.

The arrangements of the firm also comprise the supplying dinners and teas to those employed in their establishment, the cost being deducted from their wages at the end of the week, of those who are willing to be their customers. Other purveyors, however, are also allowed to send into the office.

The firm has not overlooked the claims of Religion, and a chaplain is included in the many wise and benevolent provisions made for the solid and enduring good of the little industrial army that accomplishes so much under this hospitable roof, which covers a home on a colossal scale, rather than a mere printing office.

Of the great and the permanent good that has been effected by means of the organization here observed, it is not in place to speak in detail, but it is to be wished that it were not quite in such pointed contrast to the course pursued by some firms whose principals seem to regard the working members of their respective staffs simply as so many machines, out of which the greatest possible amount of profitable work is to be wrung at the smallest possible expenditure of that necessary lubricant—wages.

Periodically the principals meet their employés here, and on these occasions it is easy to perceive how completely the wise and kindly government of the firm has rendered all as one family, having a real unity of interests, and a true reciprocity of action, fully demonstrating the practicability of even capital and labour attaining to perfectly harmonious relations.

How different is all this from what some firms exhibit, in their strained and discordant relations with the general body of their employés. The latter are, perhaps, left to work on, amid physical conditions of the worst kind, while the employers themselves, wringing from them the uttermost farthing of profit, live in the greatest material luxury. In an extreme case I have seen the reader cramped up in a little doghole of· a den, foul with evil smells, while his principal lived in a house with gilded doors and richly decorated ceilings.   It is, of course, this kind of antithesis that feeds fat the growing spirit of destructive Radicalism.

Such an establishment as that described above, quite independently of the work turned out in the ordinary routine of business, is really, so far as its practical social influence extends, a good to which the word " National " may justly be prefixed, and stands in very marked contrast to those industrial purgatories where the operatives are literally " hands," to be cast aside uncared for, and unremembered, directly they cease to be effective profit-making automata !

# IV.—HOW TO WRITE.

*How to write an Ordinary Article—Hints—How to become Invaluable as a Contributor—The Art of Writing at Will—Reference to Dr. Johnson—Words and Their Use—Slang—Authors to be Studied.*

IT seems somewhat singular that no one has yet deemed it worth while to formulise the obvious technics of ordinary article-writing. Of course, it may at once be said, that to many who, nevertheless, fancy themselves writers in an original sense, no amount of written instruction will be of avail. On the other hand, many who remember at the outset of the literary career, how much information was imparted by some kindly old Pressman, who, with a few hints and a few dashes of his pen, set crude awkward work straight, and converted it into something like " professional copy," will agree that a few good plain rules and suggestions might save many a literary tyro much needless labour, disappointment and even shame at the rejection of efforts rendered useless for the want of a little experience. In these days of universal newspaper and periodical reading, a vast amount of good plain writing has to be done which at its best is not ill paid and has the advantage of regularity, but it is not usually the object of envy to men who believe, rightly or wrongly, that they have true talent and great genius, yet it is to those who do it well, faithfully, punctually and industriously, at all events, the bread and cheese reward of Literature.

If you were writing the opening pages of a novel, you would, of course, pay attention to style and avoid tautology or clumsy sentences. Do this with your Dry-as-dust Statistics, and probably both you and your Editor will be astonished at the result. Let us suppose for the sake of a typical illustration that a Return of Railway Accidents is given you to convert into an article. Well, how would you proceed? First, you would rapidly master the principal facts as shown by the figures, and by doing this you inform yourself with, exactly what is to you in prose and matter-of-fact, all that the so-called afflatus is to the true poet in verse and matter of fancy. You have, so to speak, transferred the main facts from the Blue Book to your own brain. You have now to reproduce these facts in a readable and effective way on paper. All work-a-day Literature ultimately and necessarily, if we properly analyse the process of action, resolves itself into this. Well, you will probably find the killed and injured form a heavy list, and naturally you might begin by stating that the " Life and Limb tax on Railway travelling," using some such expression to arrest the reader's attention, now amounted to ——. This proposition laid down, very naturally you might proceed to ask : " Is this lamentable waste of human life inevitable ? " And then you would analyse the different classes of accidents and point out those which, more or less, obviously are preventible. It is surprising how soon the writer who has method, and a logical way of looking, not simply *at* but *into* things, finds

this kind of work a second nature. The fact is, all writing
of this sort comes to much the same thing as a principle,
however varied it may seem to the superficial and the unreflecting. Putting aside actually eloquent or brilliant
writing which is not now under consideration, where is
there the leading article that cannot easily be compressed
into a pithy paragraph, while in like manner most paragraph by a skilful writer, can be easily expanded into a
full sized " Leader."

In cases of special articles on persons, places or things,
more or less in the nature of monographs, the young
writer directly he has his " Subject " cannot do better
than look it up in his Encyclopædia. Having read carefully what is there written, he can generally combine with
the facts actually given him, some of those in the Encyclopædia, and as a net result should turn out a readable
article. In like manner if commissioned to visit a place of
public interest, he will do well to fortify himself by looking
up the facts of that subject in such works of reference as
he may have and reproducing thence whatever is really
pertinent to or any way illustrative or explanatory of the
particular subject. By this mode of procedure a habit is
engendered of immediately seizing on the *allusive* side, so
to express it, of everything, and to the style of the writer
who can once do this, there will always be attached the
great charm of reminding the reader of interesting things
which it is always a pleasure to have easily and naturally
recalled to us. By degrees too, the patient cultivation of
this habit of naturally fastening on the side-issues and the
real roots of everything will enable the careful writer to
so arrange the results of his own reading and personal
observation that he will always have, more or less, a rich

fund of allusion at command, and, with this ready and never failing means for illuminating his writings, he will soon be found invaluable to Editors, and although he may not have the smallest touch of genius, his " copy " will be preferential—ay—sometimes over that of far cleverer men who have never learned that mental discipline which should enable the writer to put his entire intellectual strength into any given piece of work at any given time after the " dogged " fashion of good old Dr. Johnson, who did not understand a man waiting to be in the humour to write. Genius, and equally such work as has to flow from a purely comic vein must be excepted. That kind of inspiration, for inspiration it is, no man or woman, can summon at will, but the mental power for good solid bread and cheese work—is as much at the writer's command as the disposition of any book-keeper to post up his Ledger.

Words, indeed, are to the writer obviously the sum and substance of the material whereby he becomes, so to speak, visible, and he cannot pay too much thoughtful attention to their study. Purity of style, is, unhappily not a prominent characteristic of much of the Literature of the day, and the rule of the " best word in the right place " involves too much brain-wear and tear, to suit the views of many of our temporary writers. It is true that in newspaper Literature and in much of that found in the principal magazines and periodicals of the day, really fine polished composition is not actually wanted, but the great and capital danger to the young writer is obviously the strong temptation to take for his own standard the average excellence or even less, of the contemporary Literature to which he seeks to contribute and thus it happens that the inevitable result of the mass of popular writing is as far as style is concerned, rather down than up.

Avoid slang in all cases and especially all essentially vulgar words or idioms. Of course this dictum does not apply if you are writing articles like those which distinguished the "Amateur Casual," or if you are doing dramatic fiction of any kind. Never condescend to adopt the commonplace and silly fashion of the day to clip the right names of things into what are imagined to be witty abbreviations. Thus nothing can be in worse taste or more silly than to speak or write of the International Health Exhibition of 1884 as the "Healtheries." It is pure nonsense for one thing. Let us speak and write correctly even if eloquence and grace be beyond our powers. Right, pure, and honest thinking is after all at the very root of good writing, and whenever you come upon a writer who affects slang and puts on verbal levity and resultant irreverence on every possible occasion, you may be sure that his manner of thinking is unsound, that there is something rotten about his mind and that he is not an earnest, honest, painstaking, intellectual worker. He may possibly be a wasp but certainly not a bee.

There are many admirable books on the right use of words, a thing sadly neglected in these hurry-skurry days, and it is well for the young writer to study them carefully. As a broad principle, a wide and really catholic study of all the great Poets is the best corrective to the misuse of words and especially to a vulgarity of style.

Roget's *Thesaurus* is of course an invaluable means for rapidly increasing a writer's stock of working words, but few young writers, unfortunately for their future skill, possess, or will exercise the patience to plod through such a book in an intelligent manner. Failing, however, a series of exercises that would seem but profitless drudgery to many, there can be no better reading than the Bible, Shakespeare, Milton, Pope, Tennyson, and especially Ruskin. The importance of such a course of reading early, is obvious as later in life few persons ever find leisure to do the reading that properly belongs to youth.

It were well to add really good English translations of *Tasso* (Fairfax's is the best), of Dante (Carey's), of Virgil (Dryden's, of course), of Homer and Horace and need I say of as many more of

> The great of old
> The dead but sceptred Sovereigns who still rule
> Our spirits from their urns—

as possible.

A thorough knowledge of the Bible and Bible history, Archæology and Biblical Science, is indispensable for any public writer who would reach excellence in his art, and it is, indeed, very painful to find how deplorably ignorant some otherwise well-informed men are in most matters connected with Scripture. Poetry ought to be a special study, for how can a writer properly judge of contemporary verse if he be not intimately acquainted with not only his own country's poetic classics, but also with those of the Continent, even if only through the medium of translations, such as Fairfax's *Tasso*, Mickle's *Camoens*, or Carey's *Dante*. He should, too, be a proficient in metre, and a thorough master of Prosody in its widest aspects.

He need not write verse himself, it is perhaps better not to do so, but it were as well to expect a linendraper to value aright an intricate piece of locksmith's work as to give a journalist unacquainted with metrical canons a poem to criticise, although this is but too often done. In like manner the embryo journalists must be thoroughly acquainted with Fiction, from the Romance of the Rose, or even the myths of the ancient Norse, down to Miss Braddon's latest novel. History must, of course, be read, and Buckle and Gibbon should be as familiar to him as Shakespeare and Milton. All the results of this study must be so well digested as to be immediately available. It is literary capital, and all cheques, from a penny to a thousand pounds, must, so to speak, be paid at sight. Some men, indeed, directly they tried to work on a newspaper seemed crushed by the weight of their knowledge; none of it was really available just when wanted. They required some leisure to " get up subjects," and were altogether ignorant of the fact that a journalist should be like the elephant's trunk, which picks up a pin, or a balk of timber, with equal celerity and indifference.

Encyclopædias should be systematically studied, each subject being vigorously exhausted, by means of the cross readings bearing on it, and collections of proverbs, books of quotations, and of all kinds, and especially the many short cuts to knowledge now devised for a busy shallow age, must be sedulously read, and, wherever possible, committed to memory.

These short cuts to knowledge, the ingenious means for obviating the need for independent individual thoughts, being in reality, as all sensible persons know, of little avail for the ostensible purpose of their production, will yet serve the journalist excellently well. They appear expressly designed for the newspaper writer.

A good exercise is to make a complete shorthand dic-

tionary, and another is to go through the Imperial dictionary of the English language, and write out in a MS. volume,
and very legibly, every word that you do not quite understand, and that you cannot spell or pronounce aright off-
hand.  Of course, this must be done honestly, and the result
will be a large accession to your working vocabulary, and
an excellent course of pure logical discipline to the mind.

A conscientious, painstaking student will easily improve
on these brief hints.  He will remember that the newspaper writer in these days draws his sources from all departments of human knowledge.  In the most serious leader
a clever writer may produce a marked effect by a judicious
excerpt even from *Tom Jones,* and other things being equal,
the journalist who has the largest amount of general information immediately available for daily use must always
distance all his competitors.  It is to the richness and
readiness of his allusions that Mr. Sala owes much of
his popularity.  In such a lazy intellectual age as this,
when the mass of people only make belief at work by
means of mountains of primers, technical aids, self instructors,—in a word, "cribs" of all kinds,—expressly
meant to conserve thought, by keeping it in its initial stage,
readers infinitely prefer the chatty, well-informed writer,
who talks familiarly at the point of the pen, and never
perpetrates a sentence requiring a single mental effort for
understanding it on the part of those whom he addresses.

This is the way to be popular : let your readers be insensibly led to fancy they possess the knowledge you
dispense for their amusement, and they will be grateful.

All this, however, will require time and thought in you,
and if you cannot give both, then by all means lay aside
the journalist's pen, and be content to enjoy, as a mere

reader, the labours of those who find in adroit plagiarism the shortest road to the heart of the public—that supremely wise and nicely discriminating entity. Again, if you happen to have a " wretched memory," abandon the notion of becoming a journalist. You had far better not begin a vocation which, for you, is pretty sure to end in intense misery and final failure.

One word more, newspapers readers read—being members of the public who worship that stupendous fetish of our day, the Newspaper Press,—for the purpose of *not* having to think, you must just reverse the process. *Think* about all you read, and thus acquire early the essentially important habit of instantaneous criticism. It is extraordinary, until some one points it out, what marvellous errors pass current in literature, and how helpless even educated readers in general are to detect even common blunders unless they are mere matters of ordinary grammar.

I will cite only one example, drawn from our English Homer (Sir Walter Scott), describing the personal appearance, and expatiating on the intellectual qualities of, Marmion, in Canto I. the poet says :—

> " His *square turned joints and strength of limb*,
> Showed him no carpet knight so trim,
> But in close fight a champion grim,
> In camps a leader sage."

This is a remarkably instance of an extraordinary slip in an extremely logical writer.

Marmion's square joints and muscular development no doubt indicated his powers as a formidable man-at-arms, but how could such physical peculiarities show him to be *wise* in the council? The passage is, of course, nonsense, but I never remember meeting any one who appears to have noticed the mistake—one that Scott himself would have at once corrected had anybody drawn his notice to the blunder.

Alas! this is trivial enough, I admit—mere child's play —but it carries with it, in these days, a deep, perhaps an awful, lesson. The age, like its readers, is too busy to think for itself, and its writers are fast improving on the lesson so fatally enforced by the million.

But to revert to the choice of books. One of the most able, and decidedly the most successful, editors of the London Daily Press was asked by a friend to furnish a list of books for the study of a young man anxious to succeed in journalism. He replied, "Let him read all books, by how much he falls short of fulfilling that task, will he be imperfect, as we all are!"

There is a volume of significance in this laconic reply. Long ago, and when the number of books in the world was infinitely less than now, a great student and profound thinker, devoted an elaborate essay to this very subject, and demonstrated the futility of most people's reading for culture, while in *Monte Christo* we are assured that all the true literature of the ages might be comprehended in a library of about two hundred works! In a previous section will be found an attempt to supply what may be taken as the practical bibliography of the author, and this would equally apply, of course, to the journalist. In the present instance, it will suffice to say that, for or-dinary purposes, the writer should, in addition to what may be assumed as his or her normal general infor-mation, possess a good knowledge of the principal

Greek, Roman, Oriental, and especially the Mediæval writers. Even for those " strong in languages " time will probably be saved by using good translations and edited versions, cutting down the work, and saving much needless study. English poetry should be thoroughly mastered in all its forms from the earliest period, and a fair knowledge of the stock legends and principal myths of the world is essential for any one aspiring to become a good writer, or even a reviewer on general literature. Allusion is the great charm of contemporary light literature in all its forms, and the more deeply read the writer, other things being equal, the more popular will be his productions. It is well, too, if practicable, to read a fair number of *old* books that have escaped reproduction in modern times. These are, indeed, to many, treasure houses, although it is necessary to add that the number of such works more or less unknown to the general reading public is rapidly diminishing, as there are so many industrious writers engaged in the work of virtually reproducing all that is really good from the obsolete literature of the Past.

Read, above all things, facts. It is only on a solid and extensive substratum of facts that a writer can reasonably expect to work effectively. Facts may be regarded as capital, and the skill of the writer is the means whereby those facts may be made to yield a fair rate of interest.

Above all things, let beginners cultivate a clear and most legible hand-writing.

# V.—ORDINARY REPORTING.

*What Reporting Really Is—Phonography—Practical Advice—
Effect of Habitual Reporting on the Mind—What is to be
Avoided—The late Lord Lytton—The Lefroy Case—Re-
porting Crime—A Great Evil—Anonymous Writing—The
Foreign Correspondent.*

REPORTING, as already observed, is the very base of
the newspaper proper. It is, in reality, the root
whence everything else comes, and, in nine cases out of
ten, the professional journalist has been at first a simple
Reporter.

Shorthand, then, may be considered as an indispensable
part of the equipment of every young writer for journalistic
honours, and it is a great pity that this species of writing,
so suited to the imperative needs of a feverish, combative
age, is not commonly taught at school. Learned when
young, its acquisition is not necessarily more difficult than
that of most other branches of a fair education; and then
Shorthand has a great variety of invaluable uses entirely
outside the matter of reporting.

As a rule, the embryo reporter takes to his stenographic
studies too late, when both head and hand are less pliable
than in the pupilage stage, and he usually essays his
"'prentice hand" long before he has gained any true

dexterity in an art which is very much more difficult of attainment than is popularly imagined.

On a daily, and oftentimes on a weekly journal, the duties of the Reporter are as arduous, as they are multifarious. He should be very versatile, steady, strong, active, good-tempered, and especially, must he be quick of hearing.

In shorthand writing it must be remembered that no writer can keep up with a very rapid speaker—for there are persons who will somehow manage to deliver full two hundred, and even three hundred words per minute, and such a rate of articulation is too rapid for the pen to follow, even when, as in the advanced forms of phonography, more than half the words recorded are merely indicated, and not actually written. Then, again, in general work, the Reporter has all types of character to encounter—all imaginable inflections of the human voice to attune his own brain and hand to, and all this without preparation!

In the case of Public Company Reporting, experienced reporters have no difficulty whatever, but it is vastly different where you find yourself pent up in a room amid a seething mass of the great " unwashed," clamouring, some for, and some against, the "honourable gentleman" who is about to address them ; or worse still is it in out-of-door work, where a table is a luxury not to be thought of, and where the indescribable buzz of a vast crowd smothers the niceties of the articulation of nine speakers out of ten, so that unless very careful indeed, the matter noted in your staggering, ugly strokes, hooks, circles, and dots, will be like the real speech made by Mr. Titmouse in *Ten Thousand a Year*, and absolutely defy all attempts to convert it into grammar or sense.　　　　　　　　　　　　　　　　　　　　　L

It is wonderful what verbal snares the young beginner falls into.

Many Reporters are imperfectly educated, and utterly fail to catch quotations, or even historic allusions, aright.

It is important, if practicable, to *face* the speaker. I remember on one occasion a very serious blunder was published, solely in consequence of the reporter having, through no fault of his own, his back to the speaker, whose words were, in some measure, lost to his hearing.

That indistinct, or very rapid speaking, is the cause of most of the bad reporting, of which complaint is made, is unquestionable.

Many public men in this country are wretched speakers, both as to the matter and manner, and, not being aware of the fact, cannot amend.

Some have a provoking habit of uttering rapid sequences of semi-sentences, which sound very well to the ear, but which cannot be grammatically written out, while others contract that habit of a measured utterance, mixed with a series of short syllabic gallops which defy the stenographic power of the most skilful reporter living.

Good oratory is comparatively easy to report, but the blatant periods of some are the horror of all those who have the painful duty of following them.

It might be well if speakers would occasionally remember the poor reporter, and not baffle, by thoughtlessness, his patient endeavours to keep pace with what is often but an ungrammatical gabble.

Law reporting, by reason of the great deliberation of the proceedings, is much easier, and this remark applies, too, to the police court. Here the skilful reporter should have a quick eye for character, and for minute personal peculiarities. He should be quick at hitting off prolix accounts of a variety of incidents in one or two neatly worded phrases, and he must be prompt at condensing a yard or two of rambling evidence into perhaps an inch or two of pithy report.

To the student of human nature the police courts furnish a repulsive, but an interesting, field.

They are ever-shifting kaleidoscopes of life in its most varied and antithetical aspects, and to the naturally observant, afford endless themes for profitable philosophic speculation.

The normal reporter, however, inured to the constant procession through the courts of Misery, Vice, and Crime, thinks little or nothing of the final aspects of what is to him such a commonplace scene, and, as a rule, the police reports of our leading journals are but examples of intellectual work brought by dint of much repetition to a dead level of mere mechanical detail.

This is, of course, only a negative evil.

One of a very positive kind arises out of the strong realistic tendencies of the day, which are intensified by the fierce rivalry of contending journals.

Reports are expected to be of a photographic character, and thus, however repulsive and repugnant to any true or real sense of the eternal fitness of things may be a particular case, it is frequently served up in the morning papers much as M. Zola serves up his sensual impressions of vicious Parisian life for the delectation of a multitude of impure minded persons who enjoy, above all things, that vicarious viciousness which is often more destructive of soul and body than is even actual Vice.

By the fatal fashion of furnishing a foul form of public

recreation out of the revolting records of the police courts, a kind of dry rot is introduced into the minds of many, and something infinitely worse too, than that habitual intemperance of which we hear such dire results.

Literature, in its broad aspect, as expounded by the book-writers of the age, undoubtedly elevates the tone of public morality ; but surely this is chiefly owing to the influence of a powerful criticism, and to the benign influence of those canons of true art which no book-writer can defy with impunity.

In the Press, however, we find Literature too generally at once irresponsible and utterly inartistic. Let us take an extreme case to show this clearly.

The late Lord Lytton took the well-known crime of Eugene Aram, and wrought it into a powerful and pathetic romance—much of the book is unhealthy reading—but, viewed as a whole, the main effect is unquestionably to purify and ennoble the minds of any readers not hopelessly depraved. Had Lord Lytton, however, employed his great abilities to dress up the crime exactly as the leading London daily journals dressed up the Lefroy case, his book would have been unanimously condemned by the principal reviews, scouted out of the libraries, and banished from all decent circles.

When the Press was comparatively in its infancy, and gave but bald versions of current crimes and vices, its influence on public morals was comparatively small. Now, however, that all the resources of a highly elaborated Literature are at its command, the absence of any real check on its license is a very grave evil.

Thus, for example, the attempt to shoot the Queen during February, 1882,—if it was really a serious attempt at assassination,—is a typical example of the evil referred to.

A crack-brained, miserable, starveling, snapped off a revolver at the royal carriage at Windsor, and was forthwith arrested.

In detailed history such an incident might, perhaps, claim a line, but this, of course, would never suit the tactics of some of the daily papers of the day.

Extra editions *must* be sold, and the wretched lunatic *must* necessarily be denounced with cool defiance of grammar and fact as a regicide—regicide, be it noted, is a good big word, and forms a capital piece of newspaper sensational property.

The reporters are duly inspired.

They set ardently to work, and forthwith photograph the accused with a commendable accuracy, and an intricate prolixity that would, perhaps, be comic from one point of view, if it were not so intensely exasperating to all but members of the Many-Headed Multitude.

One reporter took the culprit's coat, and remarked that "The principal part of his attire consisted of an overcoat reaching down to his knees. Once upon a time the cloth had been a dark blue colour, but is now, by constant wear, not only deprived of the nap it once possessed, but of any distinct and distinguishable colour—a dirty brownish-blue will best describe it. Its seams were threadbare, the bindings ragged, and the buttonholes frayed to a degree. This garment he wore—hiding whatever under-vestments he possessed—closely buttoned around the body, but displaying the unwashed collar which encircled his neck, or the aged scarf—once black—which half hid the nervous twitchings of his throat. His trousers were of light coloured tweed,

also considerably the worse for wear ; indeed, his boots,
—which seemed well-made, and were brightly polished,—
were the only part of his outfit that any respectable work_
man would have cared to appear in out-of-doors."

Here is historic honour for a poor, dirty, starving wretch
who ventures a random shot at the royal equipage !

One writer fastened on the bullet as a good and humorous subject, and produced the following beautiful specimen
of the English language :

" An eye-witness who was at the station, and near the
royal carriage at the time of the outrage, states that he
heard a most uncommon sound, like, as he describes it,
beer in a bottle, followed by a little crack, as of a rook
rifle, and then he saw the crowd surge towards Maclean.
From what this witness states it is most probable that the
shot ricochetted, or, in other words, rebounded from the
ground, either in front of, or underneath the carriage ; the
bullet, by the noise it made, seeming to travel slowly." (!)

Surely the " noise of beer in a bottle " is by no means
" uncommon."

The comment about the bullet seeming to " travel very
slowly," is simply nonsense, and the whole shows the
rotten nature of this sensational trash.

Another paper announced that " an expert in gunnery "
had been to inspect all the marks the bullet made, or was
imagined to have made, during its course, and then the
writer meandered into sublime speculations after the
German metaphysical model :—

" It is now thought that the ball must have gone immediately behind, or before, the body of the carriage, as had
it gone over, it would not have dropped sufficiently to hit
the truck, and, had it gone under, it would have hit the
truck lower down."

And "had it" done something else,—we might have had this kind of stuff spun out by the yard.

Then we were told that the culprit was heard "singing in his cell," and that he had eaten a "solid beef-steak," and drunk "a quart of tea" at a sitting.

Enough, surely, for that colossus, Dr. Johnson, in even his dropsical moods.

It was, apparently, impossible to exhaust the subject; one eloquent and daring descriptive Special wrote that:—

"A quite fresh mark immediately above the Queen's waiting-room was apparent, but it had no such indentation as a bullet would effect, and it was believed that it was made during the previous week when the painters were working at the roof." (!)

On the day when the cheap penny press was thus saturating itself in a deluge of twaddle, mixed with the usual vicious suggestiveness, as when one wiseacre declared with apparent exultation, as at a most benign and happy discovery, that *he* could have easily shot her Majesty as she entered her carriage, the *Times* gave less than two columns of matter-of-fact to the subject, thus setting an example to its contemporaries.

Take a file of the leading popular papers in these days, during the progress of a hideous murder trial—one which, like that of Mr. Gould, on the Brighton Railway, has been whipped up by the Press into a sensation of the day. Why anyone, however shallow, can see at once that the net result is to incite others to crime.

In addition to the tremendous publicity now accorded to the criminal, observe how the clever writers supply him with pleas, and suggest ingenious lines of defence, and point out how, if he had done this or that, instead of what he did, he could not possibly have been found guilty.

The late Lord Lytton, who was a keen observer of all popular forces, for good or evil, wrote once regarding this very subject in the following remarkable words :—

" It may be observed that there are certain years in which in a civilized country some particular crime comes into vogue. It flares its season, and then burns out. Thus at one time we have Burking—at another, Swingism— now, suicide is in vogue—now, poisoning tradespeople in apple-dumplings—now, little boys stab each with penknives —now, common soldiers shoot at their sergeants. Almost every year there is one crime peculiar to it; a sort of annual which overruns the country, but does not bloom again. *Unquestionably the Press has a great deal to do with these epidemics. Let a newspaper once give an account of some out-of-the-way atrocity that has the charm of being novel, and certain depraved minds fasten on it like leeches.* They brood over and revolve it—the idea grows up, a horrid phantas- magorian monomania ; and all of a sudden, in a hundred different places, the one seed sown by the leaden types springs up into foul flowering. But if the first reported abnormal crime has been attended with impunity, how much more does the imitative faculty cling to it. Ill- judged mercy falls, not like dew, but like a great heap of manure, on the rank deed."

Surely if the Press were a properly constituted and or- ganised Professional Body—on an exactly similar footing with any of the other liberal Professions—a marked change would come over its whole character and tone.

If the editors of the whole of the daily and weekly news- papers of the United Kingdom formed, *de-facto*, one Cor- porate body, we may well suppose that the influence of the best men among them would in the long run prevail.

There are individuals now who, if remonstrated with as to the general style of their respective journals, allege that if they changed for the better, their competitors would at once gain the decisive advantage, and they would be ruined. In truth few men are ever found really endowed with the courage of any opinion that happens to clash with the dictates of commercial prudence, but here it is obvious that the general body of newspaper editors, forming a Literary Parliament of their own, might, and should, from time to time, agree on certain common lines of action with respect to the treatment of all matters that legitimately fall within the generally accepted limits of Public Morality, Religion in its unsectarian and merely Theistic aspect, and the comity of nations. Is this impracticable ? Surely not. Consider how enormously it would augment the power of the Press for all good issues, while proportionately paralysing the existing agencies for what is distinctly evil.

Clearly, every respectable journalist ought to desire such a consummation, and once attained, how infinitely his office would gain in true dignity and genuine efficiency !

The anonymous character of English Journalism is open to many grave objections, notwithstanding many fervid advocates of the anonymous principle have brought forward much obviously special pleading on its behalf. Now, this is a matter materially affecting young writers who have their careers to run and, very generally, there is apparent a tendency to consider whether this almost universal plan of silence and secrecy, is really the best that can be adopted for the great mass of the original writing forming the substance of our ordinary Journalism.

First and foremost, it is quite certain that, as a rule,

signed articles are better written than those appearing anonymously. Many a journalist says to his secret self, " how much better I could and would write that particular article if my name appeared at the end!" Then, indeed, special pains might be taken to produce a true epigrammatic turn to this and that sentence, to hunt up authorities, and to interweave a little original thought. Special articles, although anonymous, no doubt, are especially well written, but the ordinary writing of some journals is done about as badly as it is prudent to do it by some pressmen who, if they signed their names, would certainly struggle hard to give it in their best manner and matter. From this view point the newspaper proprietor, the journalist, and certainly the reader, would all be gainers.

Then, again, would not more honesty be infused into original newspaper writing? Certainly, as one result, there might be fewer, but there would be, surely, better writers. When, for example, the Leader-writer felt that he rested rather on himself, than on the established reputation of the journal for which he wrote, he would be much more careful as to what he penned. While anonymous, he can, too often, write down rather than up, because, after all, it will be said the article appears in the *Times*, or the *Standard*, or the *Daily News*, and thence it *must* be good and great! Now, by making original writers, generally sign their names, the clever men would, undoubtedly, advance to better things, and dull and hopeless scribes would soon be excluded *in toto*.

When a Physician effects remarkable cures his name is associated with his work, and when the Barrister delivers an exceptionally fine oration, his name becomes famous. It is thus with every form of intellectual work, except

Journalism—the anonymous newspaper writer remains nameless, although his articles may become the event of the day. Then, as elsewhere remarked, now that the newspaper assumes the place and influence once solely reserved for Literature and the Pulpit, surely the nation should know who are the men who are instrumental, through the leading article, in determining to a very great extent the moral destinies of the People. Under the cover of the anonymous principle no day passes but the subtle work goes on in countless Leader-columns of sapping away the ancient foundations of Morality and Religion, and the evil, with its attendant peril, is all the greater just because it is not fully recognised. If, however, we knew (as we should if articles were signed), that the subtle assailant of Religion in the columns of some great daily journal was, after all, only the pronounced Positivist so-and-so, &c., the well-known believer in Evolution, the writings of such would be greatly reduced in their mischievous effect. No doubt Religion and generally accepted morality, are attacked so much because both are secretly treated by the mass of profligate Positivists who have made it their boast that they are quite emancipated from what they are pleased to call the idle terrors of the theological stage in the evolution of man's progress.

Practically, too, the anonymous principle is obviously preserved in the interest of the newspaper proprietor, and not at all in that of the public.

The principle, although often vehemently vindicated by men who should know better than thus to sustain what is a great injury to their own body, is incapable of any logical defence on equitable grounds.

A newspaper, let us assume, makes a great reputation,

and becomes a real power with a considerable section of the public. The result is that any writer once on the staff, if only temporarily, can, covered by this sacred anonymity, direct the entire accumulated authority and might of the paper on anybody or anything, and thus work, at times, irrevocable mischief.

If, however, he were obliged to sign what he wrote, readers would judge for themselves on the merits of the question.

It would not then be the *Times*, which says so-and-so, but simply what Mr. Smith or Mr. Brown thinks, and is permitted by the Editor to publish. If Mr. Smith had achieved a high reputation, then his views would probably be deferred to, but if he had not, he could no longer convert to his own use and purpose, the entire weight and prestige of the Journal with which he is connected. This is an important and vital distinction.

And now a brief word as to Foreign Correspondents, of whom we have heard and hear so much in these days. There are already some admirable accounts extant of their characters and services, and the world is familiar with the names of half a dozen who have won real eminence in this most difficult department of Journalism. Of course, we include here the " Special " who chronicles a campaign and, Cæsar-like, records a war ; while there are again the more stationary men who stay in some foreign capital for years, and sometimes for all their lives, mixing in Society, seeing everything that goes on around them, and acting as minute local historians of the men and manners about them, while penning political matter that may, now and then, be fraught with the destinies of Kingdoms. An able writer, Mr. William Beatty-Kingston, dealing with the subject of Foreign Correspondents says : "Of all the European realms England is the one in which, through the agency of a free, wealthy, and enterprising Press, popular interest in matters political (foreign as well as domestic) has been the most generally stimulated and developed. Englishmen of all classes bestow more attention upon the 'politics' of countries not their own, than do Frenchmen, Germans, Russians, Italians, or Spaniards, not to mention the less important European nationalities." He goes on to point out how much the English public are dependent on the information supplied by Foreign Correspondents, and states that "some of the most distinguished and efficient correspondents abroad of London newspapers were not Englishmen by birth, though, one and all, they wrote our language with remarkable force, facility, and grace. Of three of these, in particular, I may venture to say unhesitatingly that men of more shining ability or of profounder political sagacity have never been attached to the foreign staff of any metropolitan journal. I refer to General Eber, Count Arrivabene, and Dr. Abel."

The writer then sums up the characteristics of one of these typical men, Dr. Abel, of whom he says: "Finnish, Wendish, and the jargon of the 'Water-Poles' are quite as familiar to Dr. Abel as his native German, or as English, French, Spanish, Italian, Russian, and Turkish. He is, indeed, a master of twenty-three living and dead languages, including such out-of-the-way idioms as Roumanian and Basque. I have seen him write Egyptian hieroglyphics as currently as I am penning these lines ; and some years ago he published a book of seven hundred pages, having for its subject two obsolete Coptic words. Of all the learned men it has ever been my good fortune to foregather with, he is the most erudite and comprehensive."

I need hardly add that, to be a Foreign or a Special Correspondent, a good working knowledge of the principal European languages is simply indispensable.

# VI.—LEADER WRITERS.

*Leader Writers on the Daily Papers—Their Virtual Irresponsibility—Examples of Levity—Writing down to the Readers' Level—The Effect Thereof.*

THE Daily Sheet is amenable to no one and is at once above and beneath criticism. For it there can be no reviewers, although it has, broadly speaking, taken the place of books in the great work of national culture and the secret Leader Writer thus exercises an influence such as it has ever been the aim of the worst form of Jesuitism to reach. Fallacies and casuistry—misrepresentations and even immoralities which would be certainly fatal to the circulation of any conceivable book that had by some singular means got into print, pass unchallenged and uncondemned, in the morning Leaders of some Press organs. More than this, these things are as a rule read and in a vast majority of cases effect incalculable harm to the mass of men coming under the description of general readers. A writer in a daily paper, for example, makes ghastly mirth and loosely strings a number of verbal witticisms on that most appalling of all subjects that can engage the human mind—the end of the world—the joke being our planet bumping up against a comet and vanishing, squib like, in a flash of fire ! This and much more of the same kind may be repeated daily, but no voice is raised against the abomination of such writing although if such things appeared in a book, the mass of readers would at least pretend to be inexpressibly shocked. The fact is the normal Englishman has unhappily become habituated to regard his favourite daily paper as a kind of scripture and the Leader Writer as an infallible being who can never err.

People who would hardly listen to a sermon written by a Jeremy Taylor and delivered by a Mr. Bellew, will fall into raptures over the intellectual lucubrations of an anonymous Leader Writer, and, indeed, the more he writes down to their own level of thought and feeling the better they are pleased.

It may be objected that it never was a function of the Press to attempt the moral or intellectual elevation of the masses, but if we grant thus much we must add much more : it was never their right function to degrade and debase, and generally to promote the cause of selfishness, mammon, and irreligion, as so many Press organs now do.

The liberty of the Press is, or rather ought to be, quite a different thing from its license. An idea floats about and is unduly fostered by partial advocates, that suppression is always bad and that to suppress a pernicious publication must be harmful. It may do good in some particular cases, say the specious opponents of the non-intervention party, but in general it is fraught with mischief. Men are forcibly interfered with, however, when they perpetrate violence to the person—poisoners of the body are hanged if caught and convicted—but those who employ the Press as a direct medium for the propagation of vice and immorality, nearly always escape molestation.

In the House of Commons, for example, the Home Secretary had his attention drawn to an utterly atrocious and abominable publication issued in Northampton—that illustrious English town that chose in 1882 to be specially represented by an Atheist. Sir William Harcourt fully admitted that the print referred to was utterly depraved, but stated in diplomatic phrase that he could do nothing in the matter!

A chemist may not practice medicinally even to the extent of treating a simple cold—a good-natured carter may not give a poor, weary woman a ride on the high road without incurring the liability to a heavy fine—a man may not choose whether he will have his children vaccinated or not ; but Legislation, so paternal in these and a thousand other petty ways, permits hellish doctrine to be scattered broadcast and driven home by systematic lecturers and thus allows with absolute indifference, the base of the nation to be intellectually poisoned.

The true explanation of all this and of much more too, that is hopelessly wrong in our Governmental procedure is the ever increasing division which is taking place between the State and the Church. In truth, entirely separated from the Religious idea and system of rule, no code of laws can possibly be moral or just. We find clergyman, too, sharing the same suicidal delusion and some of them waiting in anticipation the approaching day when the Church of England will be disestablished. They forget that while the existing order of things remains, countries must be governed and if they aid the work of wholly secularising the government of the day, they inevitably give overwhelming preponderance to the growing party of philosophical libertines—to the band of godless scientists—to the school of utilitarian atheists—like Mr. John Stuart Mill—who will never rest content until they have tried whether they cannot entirely root out the religious idea altogether from the human mind.

The true reason why Atheism—let us not mince words and write politely of Free Thought, Secularism, Positivism, Agnosticism, or any of the utter abominations which have come in upon us like an Egyptian Plague of foul creeping things—is that the Press has, in very many instances, helped the irreligious Party might and main, and is doing so now.

Book reading is a rapidly diminishing general educational force,—popularly considered ; but some newspapers and periodicals are potent factors in the wicked crusade carried on by the leaders of the anti-God movement of the times.

Take a single instance—Evolution—had not the Press fostered this so-called discovery of sceptical scientists—had not a host of " organs " and an army of writers ardently welcomed anything that might prove the Bible to be of no authoritative force, could the thing possibly have reached its present position ? While many persons doubt what they read in books, has anyone ever questioned the accuracy of his penny paper ? Is this exaggeration ? Take the case of the Bradlaugh episode. Mr. Bradlaugh in strict accordance with his lectures, his writings and his whole public life, appeared in the guise of a Militant Atheist and strove in that character to be admitted to the House of Commons and during the whole controversy in those newspapers—by no means numerous—which professed to abominate his principles, scarcely any refer-

-ence was made to the religious character of the struggle—and after all it had no other importance—but the whole force of the writing was directed to the technical part of the strife, to its constitutional bearings and so forth. Where was there one journal that had the honesty and courage to lift up a voice that would not be silenced, against the practical blasphemy of the man, against the awful spectacle of a man defying the God who made him and seeking to trample beneath his Devil's feet all that most men are taught by their mothers to hold as unutterably sacred?

Even the religious Press was timid and half-hearted in the controversy as though it were not one on which turned issues more momentous than any that the century has known. Where Mr. Bradlaugh was denounced it was exactly on those grounds where he should have been entirely free from the smallest attack. He was reviled as a radical, and abused as a vulgar self-made man who could not put his H's in the right place.

But to revert to our subject, Leader Writers frequently form a class by themselves and moreover are sometimes solitary men enough so far as the Pressmen's convivial world is concerned. Many clever men fail curiously as Leader Writers. Some, indeed, seem from their first essay to have the true newspaper instinct and to drop into the grooves of Leader Literature quite easily. Others can never bring themselves to the right mark.

The art of saying really very little and enveloping that little in a cloud of cleverly collated, smoothly written sentences, of rising but a very little above the mental level of the average reader, and thus delicately flattering him and of leaving a good opening to fill on the next occasion—is a difficult one to acquire.

Generally speaking, the best Leaders from an Editor's view-points are poor things enough if tried by a high book standard, but they supply a demand exactly and that is the thing to be done.

Some four or five thousand Leaders and " Leaderettes " appears in these islands daily and as, if philosophically analyzed, the themes of all might be brought under a dozen heads or so, it is obviously impossible that very many of these can possess true and original literary substance. They are mostly meant for five or ten minutes easy reading and there their mission ends.

Think of the countless Leaders that have been composed in this country on one subject, say only the Eastern question and it must be at once clear that what the practical Leader Writer avoids most are two things, both to him very horrible—definiteness and finality.

The rock that even able young writers usually split on is the Essay ideal. They have Magazine papers for leading articles and use up in a column enough matter sometimes to last a professional Leader Writer for a month ! A writer of this type declared once that he had carefully thought the subject out and had reached a final issue for ever and ever.

" But don't you see that you are shutting up the subject for the paper in future? " " Well, and isn't that what you want ? " And when told that such a course would, if generally pursued, very soon bring the Journal itself to a close, our ingenuous amateur observed that a Journal which existed by keeping subjects perpetually open, was really propagating ignorance among its readers! This is but one phase of the impracticable writer from a Journalistic view-point. There are many varieties of the genus.

Ordinary Leader writing is far from difficult and especially to one having some aptitude for the work.

It needs, however, imperatively that the writer should be versatile, that his mind should be richly stored with facts of all kinds and that he should have cultivated the faculty of bringing all his intellectual powers to bear concentratedly on any given matter at any moment.

The young writer usually tides over his early troubles by what is more or less adroit plagiarism which is, indeed, by some pressmen reduced to quite a fine art.

As an instance a certain Editor habitually used a very clever contemporary which came out in the very nick of time for his purpose. One of the compositors suspected the Editor was not the true author of the crisp, epigrammatic Editorial Summary, he sent out so rapidly from the Editor's room on going-to-press days, and a boy was induced to steal the Editor's literary Prompter. The bereaved Plagiarist feared to notice the theft, he equally feared to send out for another copy of the paper and that week his paper went to press with a very bald Summary of an Index like character.

In writing a Leader, the subject forms, of course, the text and until a writer feels his strength he had better be content to open his article with some terse saying, short anecdote, some brief historic allusion to persons, places or things as the case may be. There are many neat forms of this kind which compose in truth the cut and dried stock phrases of professional writers. "Sydney Smith says," or, "if we may believe that quintessence of selfishness Rochefoucald," or again "That ferocious Satirist Dean Swift," or "Voltaire in one of his most mocking veins of Satanic irony remarks" so and so.

The setting forth of the actual substance of the Leader will necessarily occupy some space and the writer as he details his " case," will carefully note each point or salient feature on which he can remark.

In this form of literary labour practice literally makes perfect.

Everything, when the young writer has acquired some confidence, can be utilised in the Leader and the more it sparkles with allusions the better. By constantly putting your readers in mind of things they know inferentially, you give them intense gratification, as if you can say, for example, " he was all in all, a true . type of that contemporary chivalry which has been so touchingly depicted in the Colonel Newcomb of the great modern master of satire and pathos." You may find countless allusions suitable for the general article by recalling the most popular novelists of the time and the probability is that your reader, by the memory thus excited in him, feels pleasantly disposed towards *you*. This is more than half the battle and is in all ways commendable.

In this way a writer may sprinkle diamond dust over his columns and flash forth to his readers the brilliancy of true genius and by insensible degrees, he will himself be relished as the unconscious Ciceroni, of the best minds of the age. This is by no means the best form of Leader writing, but it is a mode of beginning and is better than descending to long winded disquisitions and foolish parade of what the young writer thinks—Eloquence.

In Leader writing, as in all else, the beginning is the difficulty, and where the tyro does not feel great strength, let him feel his way to better things by dealing as richly and, of course, as appositely as he can in allusions.

At first, however, the young writer may be called on to do a good deal of work which consists chiefly in adapting the writing of others to new forms and purposes. Much literary work in various publications is made to do *duty* *again* in other papers as *quasi* original matter. There are many reasons why it is not always desirable to quote the particular source of certain articles and it is understood if matter is taken over without any acknowledgment of the source whence it comes that that matter must be "worked up" anew and the more skilfully this is done the better.

Thus many class monthly publications are made up entirely out of judicious excerpts from daily and weekly papers and by judicious compression and re-arrangment a very valuable concentration of matter relative to the special object in view is secured.

To do this kind of thing very well is an art of itself. Some Journalists have consummate skill in this direction and plagiarise in such a manner that they really improve all they adopt or adapt.

In the rough and ready plagiarism, however, which is frequently part of the ordinary routine of the Journalist, the main object is to make the new version appear as different as possible from that on which it is founded and in truth strictly speaking this should not be called plagiarism, as it is rather using other writers for the information or *matter* of their utterances than for anything else, so that no question of really original writing can arise.

The following is a short example of a piece of work of this kind. It is not selected as being particularly good, but as being genuine work of the kind actually published and is therefore a sufficient example of what has to be done in this direction.

The subjoined then is a " cutting " furnished to a Sub-Editor for the purpose of founding on it an Editorial.

The original runs :

" The Inland Revenue authorities are at last really waking up and doing something to suppress the numerous clubs which are started with the sole object of evading the licensing laws and license charges payable under them. Numerous prosecutions have lately taken place and at Stafford the committees of two clubs have been convicted and fined. So long as clubs confine their operations to their legitimate members the law cannot touch them, but when outsiders are admitted at all times to these clubs and are supplied with liquor to drink and to take away, a gross abuse of the law begins and in the interests of the revenue, the general public and also of the publican, it is right that these bogus clubs should be suppressed."

Now of the above the following version was made to appear as a " note of the month " in another paper.

" Clubs and the Licensing Laws.

"It is well known that numerous so called "clubs" have been formed in various places solely with a view to evade the Licensing Laws. We are informed that the Inland Revenue authorities are at last really waking up to this fact and as a result numerous prosecutions have lately occurred and at Stafford the Committees of two clubs have been fined. While clubs limit their operations to legitimate members, the Law cannot affect them, when, however, outsiders are admitted at all times to these clubs and supplied with liquor to drink and to carry away, obviously a very gross abuse of the Law results and for the sake of all the interests concerned, it is but equitable that such bogus clubs should be sternly put down."

If the young beginner at this kind of work will go carefully through these two versions he will at once perceive
the true nature of that mill through which reprint matter
is ground into original " copy."

A ready hand at this kind of work would not by any
means need to write the above out. He would simply
strike out the words he changed and write the substitutes
in the margin ; having taken care to append or paste the
cutting on a piece of paper with a border all round of an
inch or two. In other words, he treats the reprint as a
veritable proof to be so extensively corrected that in form
it should appear quite a new thing.

A little reflection will show that strictly speaking this
adaption is not to be justly confounded with actual plagiarism as it is only the *facts* that the writer takes over
with a view of giving them a new verbal dress.

# VII.—REVIEWING.

*Reviewing—How to Review—The Necessity for General Infor-
mation—Honesty in Reviewers—A Word on Prefaces.*

ONE of the earliest tasks that will probably fall to the
share of the young Journalist is that of reviewing.
It must be confessed that this art—for at its best one may
justly so term it—has not advanced, but has rather declined
with the multiplying of more or less critical organs and
for reviews, we should rather in many cases read simply
" notices " of books.   One cause of the evil is that books
are now frequently placed in the hands of ignorant men
and to these insufficient time is allotted, and as in numerous
cases, the books have to be returned and no extra fee is
paid for the so called "Reviews," what can be expected?
The amount of general information, to say nothing of
culture, learning, and a power of mental analysis, imperatively needed in a Reviewer, if he is to review properly, is
very great.   In high class and well conducted Journalism,
the more important works are usually given out to proved
writers who are known to possess, at least, a good acquaintance with Literature, and a judicious Editor appor-
tions the work to his knowledge of those in whose hands
the work is placed.

For one thing, however, in these high pressure days

when men come to the surface from many other causes than merit, there are so called smart young Journalists to be met with in plenty, who are almost entirely, so to speak,. nineteenth century men. That is they possess only a very vague idea of the classics, and of the older forms of Literature they know absolutely nothing beyond a few names. and dates. We remember one of this type perfectly puzzled in a reprint of Herrick, over the passage in which the poet gaily sings :

> Some asked how pearls did grow and where—
> I pointed to my girl
> To part her lips and show them there
> The quarrelets of pearl !

The gentleman referred to had never seen a quarrel— the bolt of the old crossbow—with its square shaped head and was quite astonished, when reminded that the poet referred to the ammunition of the crossbow.

This is only a sample, however. In the matter of reviewing it is obviously important that the Reviewer should possess good general information, but here it is that so many lamentably fail.

Then again, apart from the question of information there is that of honesty. The young Reviewer when a book is put in his hand for review should feel that his duty requires him to ascertain simply what the writer means, and how he has expressed his meaning and to convey to the readers of the Review as accurate an idea of what the book *is*— not what the reviewer may think it is, as a matter of bias or prejudice—as his power of analysis will admit of.

Let anybody glance at any number of Reviews of the eighteenth century and he cannot fail to be struck with the fact that as expositions of the books dealt with, they were much superior to most of the slipshod, slovenly misleading notices which comprise more than half the so-called Reviews of the present day.

The cardinal principle to be observed then by the young Reviewer is *what* does a book say, and *how* is it said ; that formula includes everything. Another thing is that many Reviewers, if such they can be called, content themselves with looking at the title and contents of a work and then proceed to " evolve " their criticism, while others again follow at their elbow the cutting of reviews that have already appeared and deliberately plagiarise them simply to save themselves trouble ! Such a course is doubly dishonest and wrongs both Publisher and Author.

Let the young Reviewer determine from the first that he will actually *read* what he is set to criticise. By "reading " it is not meant of course, that he must needs pore over every line, but let him turn the pages over, and by practice he will soon be enabled to " take in " the meaning of each ordinary book-page at a glance, and will soon know when he ought to read and when to skip. At present in thousands of cases there is no thought at all of " reading " and even " skipping," is applied only to a small part of the whole, and many of the perfunctory Reviewers of the day will, as they sometimes express it, " take the chances " of being called to account, which virtually they never are in any really effective manner.

Surely it follows that newspapers, if writers signed their articles, would necessarily be compelled to obtain and if possible, retain really able and conscientious Reviewers if they desired to remain powers, whereas now, once a paper has made a name, much of the work may be, and is, done by men who, if deprived of the Editorial "we," would be found of but little account as our intellectual guides.

The signing of original matter would also infuse very much honesty and truth into that department of the Press which actually forms what is known as Public Opinion.

Writers when anonymous, do strange things that would never be even possible if they had to identify their writings and thus the entire tone of the Press would inevitably be elevated and greatly purified.

Let us take a typical case. A new writer sent a volume containing much original matter—the matured work of many years of careful thought, to a leading Review. In due time a notice appeared in which the reviewer stated " that he could only give the author credit for his skill in packing," and so dismissed a production pronounced by competent authorities to be meritorious, with a sneering pleasantry. The result was that the Review in question, an acknowledged authority, had dammed the book but had the writer been obliged to sign his verdict he might have hesitated at identifying himself with a judgment founded either on gross ignorance or malicious prejudice. Either he had read the book and was resolved to injure it so far as he could, or he had not read it and to save himself trouble, substituted a paltry play of words for a proper criticism.

As to Reviewing in general it is only possible to throw out a few hints.

The Reviewer is too apt to think principally of himself and very little of the author. In old-fashioned days the Reviewer was more inclined to fulfil faithfully his natural and proper function of *book-taster* and reported on each work submitted to him, accordingly.

In those cases it was the *book* that appeared in the Review, bitter or sweet according to circumstances, now it is the *Reviewer* in general with just a little dash of the author to give colour and some consistency to what is too often a sham.

The simple test to apply to a book should be what is done here and how it is done. Honest answers obtained by an adequate examination of the book will yield a fair criticism. As things are, the Reviewer is only thinking of himself and is asking all the time—how can *I* shine out—how can *I* look clever, smart and witty? this is intensely vicious and utterly ruins the value of nine-tenths of the criticisms of the day.

Then there are a good many lazy critics, men who will not think about their work, but who go entirely by the name and repute of the author, and praise or blame accordingly as these are famous or obscure.

They have two or three rough and ready formulas and just enough instinct to keep clear of any absolutely egregious blunders and they go on their way reproducing in other words old criticisms and dealing out praise and censure according to what they assume to be the worldly standing of the works and men with which they arbitrarily deal.

Let the young Journalist beware of dropping into anything of the kind. Let him read what he criticises and, above all, let him remember that truth and candour are worth infinitely more than all the wit and satire in the world.

Preface-writing, by-the-way, is often an anticipative veiled method of prejudiced or partial Reviewing, designed to bias the reader and, if possible, disarm the critic, although, in this latter respect, success is but rarely attained. As a rule, the " Preface," or " Introduction," is a mistake and had best be left out, or if, as occasionally occurs, either one or the other is rendered absolutely necessary, let the exordium be brief and pithy, and as business-like as possible. Some writers, by-the-way, adopt a far too apologetic style and actually condemn their own work, being anxious, apparently, to be before their Reviewers in this respect. This, of course, is a blunder; and equally so, but in worse taste, are the jaunty, self-conscious prefaces which appear now and then, wherein the author pretends not to care for the Reviewers, and expresses a withering scorn of all critics of whom, all the while, he is most likely in mortal terror. In general, the Preface is quite as much open to objection as the excessive use of foot-notes. In point of fact, " after thoughts " are practically, more or less, corrections, and ought, properly, to be embodied fully in the text *prior* to publication, as otherwise the author is virtually revising his work in public, and this, surely, is a thing to be avoided. That Prefaces are often untrustworthy may readily be guessed, and, as throwing some curious light on this point, I extract a communication made to the *Athenæum* of March 6th, 1886, by Mr. Richard Edgcumbe, entitled " Behind the Scenes," in which he says that it was his fortune to pick up at an old bookshop an uncut copy of *Greece in* 1823 *and* 1824, containing the letters of Colonel Leicester Stanhope, with a Preface by the Editor, Mr. Richard Ryan. While in the act of cutting the leaves Mr. Edgcumbe found a manu-script, unsigned and undated. The caligraphy is in the style in vogue during the first half of the present century, while its substance obviously relates to the terms of the

Preface which Mr. Ryan was instructed to write. It runs
as follows:—

### "Heads of Preface.

"Eulogize the Greek Cause and the exertions of Stanhope, and show the apparent certainty of the Greek Cause
becoming Victorious.

"State the Probable Progress the People have made in
Literature and Civilization by means of the Presses established by Col. S. during the Conflict.

"*Blaze away* about the Greek Cause appealing to the
Breast of every Englishman, and wind it up with showing
the Greek Cause to be of permanent importance to every
body who has any right ideas of decency and propriety.

"State the usual lie of the Publication being undertaken
more with a view of serving the Greek Cause than of
profit, and *splash* away about 5,000 other fine things
which just now I can't think of.

"Mem: If Lord B. is spoken of let him be praised, and
*gammon* us well about his loss to the Greek Cause. I think
a slight *Buttering* of the Greek Committee would not be
amiss. And if, in speaking of Stanhope, you choose to
bring in what the *London Magazine* says, I think it could be
well introduced."

These instructions, as may be presumed, were very
faithfully carried out. This, doubtless, is only a small
sample of much work of the same kind, and suggests how
interesting it would be could we only come across some of
the original letters of advice and instruction sent to De Foe
when he was engaged, in profound secrecy, as a political
and partisan writer to the Government of the day.

# VIII.—THE WORKING JOURNALIST.

*His Qualifications—How and What to Read—The Sub-Editor
—A Real Day's Work on a Weekly Newspaper—" Making
Up."*

THE qualifications requisite to constitute a really good
practical journalist are many and various.

Primarily, the journalist should be constitutionally, if
not physically, strong, and should be able, when occasion
demands, to dispense with sleep, as well as to take it at
any time and in any place, when needed, after the plan of
the Great Napoleon, who, it is well-known, *willed* slumber
at his convenience.

The practical journalist should have a perfectly even
temper, and if not himself humorous, should be capable of
appreciating humour.

He must know absolutely everything, or rather *seem* to
know, that being the true journalistic art, and he should
be a complete cyclopædia, ready at the shortest notice to
turn on a stream of exact and perspicuous knowledge on
any subject within the possible range of the "general
reader," to the extent of from half-a-dozen terse lines to
as many columns—if need arise.

He must be, and that often with kaleidoscopic rapidity,
a profound jurist, an acute special pleader, a sound divine,

a subtle casuist, a bluff soldier, a sentimentalist, an æsthetic enthusiast, a book-worm, a plain matter-of-fact exponent of the common-sense realistic school, or possibly a dogmatic Doctor of Laws.

At times, he may have to be a statist, a produce merchant, a stockbroker, and, in a word, must, like Shakespeare himself, exhibit practical knowledge of every vocation in life.

He must appear to be a skilled engineer, a ready mechanic, a competent judge of pictures and old china, and perhaps, at times, he may have to pronounce on ladies' dress.

He may at all events have, without warning, to take up the subjects of any of these vocations and industries, and to write more or less pointedly on each.

As to general information, the journalist should be well read in all literature past and present.

He should have at his pen's point neat, well turned summaries, and luminous expositions of all the accepted, and many of the rejected, philosophic schools of thought of the world.

He should be equally ready and competent to discourse in a popular and original manner on Confucius, Luther, or Comte.

He must know his Plato, and have a speaking acquaintance with the Koran and the Talmud.

He should know what Duns Scotus taught, and have some acquaintance with the poetry of Hafiz.

In geography he must be very exact, and on seeing a bare name in an obscurely worded telegram should know at once under what heading to put the news.

It is well for him to be something of a natural philosopher, and to understand comparative grammar. If he is personally skilled in music and painting so much the better.

He should understand the rudiments of agriculture, the general outline of staple manufactures, the main principles of commerce, and as much as may be—being an Englishman—of maritime and colonial affairs.

Does even this exhaust what is necessary for the really typical journalist? Oh! no, indeed! There is more even yet. He should know something of Athletics, and have an outline knowledge, at all events, of the principal national games and sports of his own and of foreign countries.

He should understand all games of chance or skill, and be well versed in the unwritten canons of good society.

Even then, assuming him to possess this mass of information, he should have especially the master faculty of immediately and accurately applying any required portion thereof to any subject or topic under the sun, at a moment's notice, and he must know how to stop quite naturally, if need be, and the printer informs him that there are so many lines too many.

All this mass of general information is to be available then at any time, and without definite notice.

The working journalist may be bilious, he has a splitting headache, or a fever in his throbbing arteries; no matter that, the printer cannot wait, and he must supply the " copy."

One nearest and dearest to him is desperately ill; no matter again, the press will not stop, and the really successful working journalist—the man who is ultimately sure to rise—is he who approximates most nearly to a kind of human organ, provided with innumerable stops for all possible occasions. Thus it comes about that at last the various required literary themes are ground out with entire indifference as to whether it be a paragraph touching a missing child, or a resounding trenchant leader on the Franchise.

The one golden rule is for the young journalist to be determined to write his very best whenever he *is* writing, and never to fall into the fatal error of reserving what he supposes to be " his superior powers," for what *he* deems a worthy occasion.

The work of the present moment must always be done well, and this habit once acquired, ultimate success, sure promotion, and, perhaps, the prize of fame itself, are all within a measureable distance.

And now a word as to the manner of gaining, in some degree, the qualifications mentioned above as necessary (and they are in a great degree) to constitute a working and really practical journalist.

Well, at starting, most capable young Englishmen having brains, will have many of these qualifications, which appear unduly formidable, from being concentrated in this short summary thereof.

The more he knows at first hand, from actual experience, from work, and from direct sources, the better, the rest, so far as possible, must be the outcome of really thoughtful reading—of a strong memory, a good judgment, and especially the early acquisition and constant practice of a thoroughly perspicuous mental organization. A bad memory is almost fatal to a journalist, but then that would be so, too, to many other vocations.

The journalist should seek to " qualify " somewhat as a rising barrister reading in chambers does for *his* profession, and it must never be imagined that much preliminary reading can be well dispensed with.

Once at work, there is little, if any, time for continuous reading, and more time is spent over bad proofs than can be given to books.

Among the more indispensable books wherewith the young writer should, if possible, provide himself, may be cited the following : *Haydn's Dictionary of Dates, Bartlett's Dictionary of Familiar Quotations, Cruden's Concordance* for the Bible, and a Concordance to Shakespeare. *Wheeler's Noted Names in Fiction,* and *Familiar Allusions* are good books to have, together with the following : *Adam's Dictionary of English Literature, Brewer's Dictionary of Phrase and Fable,* and *Walford's Men of the Time.*

So far as I am aware there is no book which really describes the purely technical aspect of a sub-editor's normal work.

It happened in my own case that I obtained the post of sub-editor very early indeed in my career, and I can well remember, even now, the many frights I had, due to my want of technical knowledge, which might have easily been obviated had I had access to a good Manual in the work before me.

It is a serious thing for the young journalist, known as yet to one journal only, to lose his situation, and brevet rank, for some technical error, too serious, perhaps, to be overlooked, and yet easily avoided by one who knows the technical routine of the Newspaper Press.

In general, editors and newspaper proprietors too, are sufficiently human to render such a disaster as dismissal rare, but the young journalist will seriously delay his upward progress, and diminish his prospects of increased emolument, if he disdains to study attentively all the mere details of his work.

The fact is, that the finish and standing of a journal or periodical, depends very much more than is generally supposed on the sub-editing, and thus, in newspaper economics, the sub-editor is an all important factor.

Let us now take in detail a real day's work, such as I have often myself done, in getting ready the " copy " for a good weekly normal family newspaper.

As early in the morning as practicable, I obtained all the daily London morning newspapers—generally I took six—*The Times, Standard, Daily News, Daily Telegraph, Morning Post*, and *Daily Chronicle.* Laying these flat, one on the other, I turned their pages, and, with scissors, cut out all the news items I wanted, going steadily through the whole until every item of news of real importance or popular interest was eliminated.

" Well," says some amateur, " there does not seem much that is technical in that operation ! "

Pardon me, I have skeletonised those six papers in a trifle over thirty minutes (the work can be done in less on a pinch), and there is not an item of intelligence of any kind, from the Report of a bank meeting, buried in the odds and ends of a city article, to a good point in a Leader, that has escaped me.

I have now a pile of most miscellaneous cuttings (those turning one column being gummed or pasted to their respective continuations), including all the brilliant bits, or nearest approaches thereto, in all the six morning daily journals.

Sitting down, I proceed to reduce this chaotic mass of literary chips and shavings into order.

As only one subject should be placed on the same piece of paper, it is best to have a pile of copy paper, of note size, and to fix on each sheet the cuttings. I then edit each cutting with a pen just as they come from the pile on my left, to be bestowed in another pile on my right, fit for the compositor—if ultimately passed for "copy." The "editing" consists in substituting for "yesterday," wherever it occurs, the date of the month, or the name of the day, and in "cutting down" verbiage,—well enough in a daily report, but not wanted in a weekly journal, where space is precious. Thus, while writing these pages, I look in a daily paper for a short example of how to cut down and I read in "this day's police" that "a man giving the name of so-and-so, was charged," etc. Well, I should instinctively make that, with a touch or two of the pen, "a man named," or, perhaps, merely say "William So-and-So." As a rule, the reprint copy can be reduced, *i.e.*, compressed, with great advantage, and turned into better English, too.

Practice, alone, will make this work a second nature, and a kind of instinct will be ultimately acquired which will enable the young journalist to know exactly where and when to alter.

Much time is saved by adopting the promiscuous order with the cuttings as they are gummed, or pasted, to the slips of copy paper.

Here comes a sensational murder, and now a wedding in high life for the Court and Fashion heading, and now again a special piece of political news for the Foreign Intelligence, which is rarely original in weekly journals.

Great care must be taken to descriminate final from pending news. Unfinished cases should be put aside for reference, and for such additions as the next day's news may involve. Some of these cuttings are put by merely to serve as hints, or as subject matter for editorial notes, leaders, "chat" notes of the day, gossip, jottings, or whatever may be the specific headings of the editorial sections of the Paper to be made up.

The nett outcome of the combined work of scissors, paste, and pen, is, that in a surprisingly brief space of time, I find myself in possession of a stout little unbound volume, containing all the news of the day, deprived of all superfluous verbiage, and roughly fit for " copy."

In a smaller pile are the monitors that furnish hints and cues for " original " matter, the texts,—in short, for the lay sermons of the sub-editorial department.

I am by this time, as may be inferred, fully posted up in all the news of the day, and the next step with a systematic working journalist, is to write such original matter as may be safely composed without fear of its main assertions being upset by later news.

These combined operations have taken from two to three hours, and I remember feeling after each "turn" of this kind very much as I imagine an engine driver does when he has driven an express train through half-a-dozen junctions at fifty miles an hour.

Literally I have had to tear myself intellectually through a mass of matter (omitting advertisements) of, say, some hundred columns of news, and comment thereon.

In one paper I have seen a statement, which another contradicts,—a fact I instinctively note—here I find an item perilous to reproduce, for it is the germ of that terror to all respectable journalists—a libel,—there I have found an expression unfit for reproduction in a " family " paper, and in other places I have detected, and at once corrected, sundry blunders.

It will be readily allowed that severe preliminary self-mental training is necessary to enable any one to sweep over such an expanse of miscellaneous matter, and to select thence, without capital errors, exactly what is really required, rejecting all that is worthless for re-production in a well edited, *i.e.*, sub-edited, weekly news-sheet. The editor, in point of fact, has nothing to do with this preliminary process, and judges the work of the sub-editor not in detail, but solely by the whole result.

The eye-training for this kind of work is a matter of time, of course, but he who is quick and apt, will soon feel surprise at the rapidity wherewith he can sweep the sheet of a daily paper, and take in the general headings, subjects, &c., at a glance. Judgment is an essential condition of this kind of work, and it should be tempered by uniformly good taste—the second nature of a properly cultivated mind.

Sometimes, as for many years in my own experience, the news is derived from an incoming batch of papers by mail, and a whole number has to be got up and put to press just as soon as possible. In my case, I took two copies of each important mail paper, as all valuable news matter had to be reproduced, and good items often lay at the back of other matter cut out of " copy." I would simply lay the papers two by two on each other, taking, of course, page 1 of number 1, and page 2 (at the back of page 1) of the duplicate. For, as already explained, all " copy " must be on one side of the paper only.

This, though much, does not by any means exhaust the work of the sub-editor.

Let us take a miscellaneous parcel, such as has been

sent to my home from the office on days of non-attendance there, and designed to furnish, more or less, matter for the readers of the family newspaper in question.

Here, then, are my "exchanges," a motley group, including journals from the Provinces, America, the Colonies, and abroad generally,

There are "letters to the editor," books for Review, long, and often ill-written, letters on ridiculous or, perhaps, wholly foreign subjects, as far as the scope of the journal addressed goes, from readers who have "found me out," in a geographical, or, perhaps, an astronomical blunder, and who, with an exquisite kindness, now communicate their discovery.

There are "privately printed" pamphlets, statements of the wrongs of this gentleman or that lady—terrible accusations against the Commander in Chief by some ex-army officer who has a permanent feud with the War Office, and generally quite enough matter to thoroughly wreck the journal with law-costs and fines, to say nothing of imprisonment for the editor, if only half were thoughtlessly published that is so kindly, trustfully, and generously contributed by outside friends burning to air their grievous wrongs in a newspaper.

Tickets for theatres and concerts, for meetings of scientific societies, invitations to see new and wonderful patents, to report on a Manchester goods warehouse, or to inspect a soap works, tumble out with petulant complaints from subscribers who have moved, and marvel why they do not get their copies all the same, and who will never learn that they should address the publisher, and not the editor, on such a subject.

Then there are books for review, treatises on chemistry,

or algebra, amateur poems, and trade "puffs" in pamphlet form.

There may also be a few charmingly candid letters from persons who condescend to praise my paper and excellent articles, but some numbers ago—they do not quite remember when—in some part of my "valuable impression, they do not quite remember where," they saw something about a cure for ear ache, and now send me twopence, and would I kindly oblige by sending them the particulars!

"Ay!" they say, or think, "he has his scissors ready, and makes a file of the paper his pillow by night and his seat by day. He can soon snip out what we want, and don't forget we sent twopence!"

Surely such an avalanche as this—and I do not exaggerate, as I have lived through such literary stress for many years—would be a little—just a little—perplexing to some of my readers? And especially to such as have gathered from Mr. Anthony Trollope that an ink-pot, a pen, and a quire of paper are really all that is needed to set up the modern journalist!

Well, somehow or other, without losing my temper, or overlooking one of these very miscellaneous items in the above-mentioned parcel, I have ploughed my way through the pile.

I send some of the tickets to persons specially qualified for the work involved in their use; I endorse such letters as are meant for the publisher or his clerk, and, perhaps, hint an answer in a few rapidly scrawled words in the margin.

I review most of the books there and then, including the amateur poems, whence some fun may, perhaps, be extracted, as on one occasion, when a young Bard of Epic aspirations wrote in grandly flowing lines of the "small gilt clouds" that attended the "dying God of Day."

I steer very carefully clear of all those kind ladies and gentlemen whose ardent desire it apparently is to lead me to publish criminal libels on some one of whom I know nothing, about a matter entirely inexplicable, and find at last that my labours and the evening have finished together.

I have worked in an intellectual mill like a galley slave, and have earned that day's pay at the rate of from £250 to £300 a year.

These days are varied by seeing the paper to press, by occasionally writing essays and magazine articles—if an opening presents itself for such—by visiting places that require personally inspecting, and by generally promoting the interest of the journal represented in every possible way.

"Making up," as it is technically called in the printing office, is apt, at first, to dismay the young journalist the first time he is required to superintend this operation.

In point of fact, it is both simple and easy, and need cause no special anxiety to any one who keeps himself cool and judicious. The printers themselves do the really troublesome portion of the work.

The various items, great and small, forming the journal or periodical are laid up in type in long galleys, which resemble long narrow trays, while others intended to hold the two or more columns, constituting a page, are made of proportionate width. The foreman printer, or his deputy, furnishes the editor, or whoever may be appointed to superintend the "make up" of the publication, with a written statement of quantities, which may run thus—I cite a real estimate :—

| | |
|---|---|
| Editorials . . . . . . | $5\frac{1}{2}$ |
| Leaders . . . . . . . | $2\frac{3}{4}$ |
| Law . . . . . . . | 4 |
| Crime . . . . . . . | 8 |
| Accidents . . . . . . | 6 |
| Music and the Drama . . . . | 2 |
| Reviews . . . . . . . | 2 |
| General Intelligence. . . . . | 4 |
| Correspondence . . . . . | 1 |
| Our Serial Story . . . . . | 4 |
| Advertisements . . . . . | 10 |
| | $49\frac{1}{4}$ |

Wanted, 48 columns.  $1\frac{1}{4}$ excess.

You have here—this is a very easy case—to mark off as " hold over," $1\frac{1}{4}$ columns, and in doing this you have to consider what may be " held over " until the next number of the publication with the least loss to the current issue and with the greatest probability of being fit for use thereafter.

You know at once that certain items must appear, but you will see at a glance that there are other items which will " hold over " and these you must indicate to the Printer, giving him at the same time the sequential order of the make up.  In doing this you will, of course, be guided by the general character of the publication, by specific instructions, information, and the like.

Sometimes it is found that a particular article falls awkwardly and you may be asked to supply a few words or lines to fill out a given space or to reduce an article.

All these and many similar matters come naturally and readily from the Printing office.

The young beginner will invariably find Printers ever ready to give every possible aid, provided only they are treated with proper consideration and are not needlessly "worried."

Printers, in truth, are a much enduring, long suffering race, and deserve all the kindness that Editors, "Subs," and others engaged in practical Literature can extend to them.

# IX.—NEWSPAPER PROPRIETORS.

*Newspaper Proprietors—Sketches of Some—Their Characteris-*
*tics—What Journalists have to contend with—A Striking*
*Example.*

NEWSPAPER Proprietors are naturally of infinite
variety, but roughly, they may be classed into those
who take little or no part in the conduct of their Journals,
and those who are never contented without putting one
finger and sometimes their whole hand into the Editorial
pie.

The late Sergeant Cox was a model for all really judicious Newspaper Proprietors. He was very difficult to
please in the first selection of an Editor, but when once
chosen, he never interfered with the work in the slightest
degree. So punctilious was he that it is related of him
that he never sent a certain book of his to one of his own
Journals for review, and being rallied on this by a friend
said, with the greatest simplicity, that he did not wish it to
be unfavourably reviewed! He knew the character of
his Editor and his Editor would most certainly have dealt
with the book as with one of an utter stranger.

All honour to a man who could act like this and who
could cluster around him, as he undoubtedly did, men of
high honour and solid principle!

The result is, in far too many cases, that the Press suffers severely from the utterly injudicious and sometimes un-principled meddlings of the Proprietorial with the Editorial powers.

I knew one Editor some years ago who was forced reluctantly to decline some extraordinary correspondence offered him from Central Asia, because, his rich Proprietor dreaded the effect that such matter might have on certain stock in which he was interested. It is quite possible for a newspaper Proprietor to bring the overwhelming weight of his own personal investment in a certain stock to bear on his Editor and thus convert his paper into a gigantic agency for the inflation of public securities which may ultimately prove worthless.

To do the Press justice when nefarious things are done in this way, it is much more likely to be the work of the Proprietor than of the mere Pressman.

Unfortunately it is often practically impossible for the Editor to fight his Employer on grounds of equity, and, if a man of real principle, he has to resign, and this is a serious matter as the Editorial chairs of the Daily Journals are extremely difficult to obtain and even a good man once fairly ousted may easily find himself compelled to sink into a subordinate position. This, by the way, is an evil that could be met by an association of Pressmen as such points could be submitted to the council if a Proprietor attempted to act summarily and the council decided that he was in the wrong, he would find it impossible to obtain any properly qualified Editor inside the association.

Such a knowledge and the certainty that all underhand proceedings directly they reached dimensions possibly affecting the general public, would be duly reported to the central body, would have a wholesome effect.

Some Proprietors are simply meddlers and muddlers by virtue of an uncontrollable propensity to interfere in anything in which they have concern. I know one Editor who had a Proprietor of this type who made his life a kind of Purgatory for several years. My friend was equally good natured and prudent, but weak, and he unfortunately too often gave way. In this case the Proprietor had a great idea of his refined taste in composition and even the Leaders of the *Times* did not always satisfy his extreme fastidiousness. The whole thing was of course absurd.

The readers of a newspaper do not look for, or, as a rule, in the least appreciate extreme refinement of style, with them the matter is everything, the manner is of minor importance, if only it be fluent and intelligible. This extreme critical Proprietor would waste valuable time and often occasion expensive and most inconvenient corrections merely to alter the paragraphing, the punctuation or the adjectives of a piece of anonymous writing that was to live for a day. His newspaper failed but it failed in the odour of Propriety and was a delightful sample of what I may term cast iron composition. Its general faultlessness was its great fault and it died at last, like some human beings do of too much medicine and surgery.

The wise newspaper Proprietor, like the late Sergeant Cox, leaves the Editor as free as possible. No Proprietor can understand a Journal like the man who conducts it. You might as well bawl instructions to the huntsman when he is scouring the field as to how he shall guide his horse.

Whenever the Proprietor begins to act the part of Editor, ruin impends over the Journal unless, indeed, he have the ability to become his own Editor. The truth is no paper can go with two Editors. The result is sure to be disaster as it was when the Romans attempted to fight Hannibal by sending against him two Consuls of equal authority.

These remarks, of course, rather affect the Journalist than the Public, although even there they have their significance especially in days like these when the great mass of the nation is permeated with a most absolute faith in the general infallibility and consummate wisdom of the Newspaper Press.

*Ancient origin of Comic Literature—Jesters and Court Fools—*
*The Charivari and Punch—The Colonial Comic and Illus-*
*trated Press—Evil tendencies of some Illustrated Journals—*
*Bills and Posters.*

THE Comic and the specially Illustrated Press form
features and forces of the periodical Literature of
the day which ought not to be passed over without some
mention in a work like this.  The origin of the former is
remotely ancient, and in Aristophanes, for instance, we
find the real beginning of much that is now put forth,
enriched by pen and pencil, far beyond the utmost conception of the classic Fathers of modern Wit and Humour.
Then, again, throughout the whole of the mediæval period
we can trace in the strolling Jesters and "Fools," as well
as in those who were permanently attached in a singular
kind of not disagreeable servitude to the Courts of
sovereigns and the semi-regal state of great nobles, the
rude ancestors of our masters of verbal fun and grotesque
fancy..

The "mummers" and Wandering Players of Chivalric
Europe were the true precursors of the Tom Hood's, the
Mark Lemon's, and other humourists and wits of our own
day, and truth was uttered in jests at times when its serious

enunciation, unless sustained by physical force, was commonly fatal to the man who dared to think for himself.

In a word, the Comic Press of our own times crystallizes, so to speak, the wit and wisdom which ranges from Æsop himself to the Dick Tarleton and Will Somers of Shakespearean England. This, in truth, opens a curious question as to the way in which the objective life, the true men and the real manners are being continually crystallized in succeeding literary thought, so that, in a certain sense, each passing phase of human action on the great stage of the world is, in due course, embalmed in the current intellectuality of the age.

Court Fools, undoubtedly, existed from the earliest times of nascent civilization. Dionysius of Syracuse, Augustus Cæsar, and other classic sovereigns maintained men about them to enliven their tables with pleasantries, for the ancients understood well how much a laugh aids digestion; and later came the professional "fool," with shaven head, the cap furnished with asses' ears, the mock sceptre, and all the rest of the motley array that we find in mediæval pictures. Among famous historic "Fools" were Triboulet, Jester to Francis I. of France; Klaus Narr, who flaunted at the Court of Frederica the Wise of Prussia; and Scogan, the Fool of our own pleasure-loving Edward IV. English Court Jesters died out with the Stuarts, the last being Achie Armstrong who, curiously enough, died appropriately, it was said, on April 1, 1646.

These men unknowingly laid the foundations of the Comic Press to follow.

In England, Caricature, as a distinct literary entity, came into full being with the famous drawings of James Gilray who, between 1779 and 1811, issued 1200 spirited caricatures relative to contemporary events, and undoubtedly led the way to the establishment, some time later, of the initial Comic and Illustrated Press as we now understand it.

The English *Punch*, founded in 1841, was anticipated by the famous *Charivari*, established in Paris in the year 1832. Charivari is a term employed in French to signify a discordant tumult, such as might be produced by the rough music wherewith rustics used to aid the bees in swarming, and it indicates also a wild commotion of bawling, groans, and hisses, the inarticulate utterance of a furious and maddened mob. The etymology of this most expressive word is very obscure indeed. The German equivalent is *Katzenmusik*, and in English we have a good rendering in *Caterwauling*. It has been compared, indeed, to the "marrow bones and cleavers" which formed at one time the customary concerts gratuitously provided by satirical neighbours at vulgar weddings, and where there was a marked disparity in the ages of the bride and bridegroom.

The English *Punch*, it is needless to say, soon became a recognised Literary Power, and has long since been recognised as an institution, a true censor of men and manners, and, in almost every instance, a power wielded on the side of Right, Truth, and good Morals. Of recent years a corresponding Comic Press has grown up in the Australasian Colonies, and there we have a Sydney and a Melbourne *Punch*, published respectively in the capitals of New South Wales and Victoria, and dealing with Colonial men and manners, much as *Punch* does here. Of late the Comic Press, with its numerous distinct satirical off-shoots, has very greatly developed, and, on the whole, has made very great advances. No species of current Literature, probably, makes such severe demands on the brains of its producers, and with each year the difficulty of finding new ideas becomes, naturally, greater and greater.

The Illustrated Press has, obviously, followed the enormous diffusion of art among the mass of the people. Painting and Sculpture still remain, to a great extent, the luxury of the rich and leisure classes, but the cheap Illustrated Journal ministers to the inate æsthetic cravings of the million and, with some few exceptions does so in this country, in a pure and noble manner. That the tendency is strongly towards a far greater development of the Illustrated Press is palpable enough. There is, evidently, a strong disposition to illustrate daily newspapers, and, on many occasions, of late years, this has even been done in a crude and fitful manner. It is much to be feared, however, that when Science has discovered the means now eagerly sought for—the reproduction, at the shortest notice, of an artist's sketches—that the effect will be to vulgarise many journals by pandering to the morbid desire, so evident in the mass, for sensational details, as to all events in the vast world of Vice and Crime, which is allowed, unfortunately, to cast up so much of its foul foam in the columns of even our leading journals. Otherwise the expansion and greater elaboration of the Pictorial principle in periodical literature would, unquestionably, be a happy thing, and one that would surely help on the intellectual culture of the mass of the people.

It is noteworthy, by-the-way, that the contemporary Australasian Press, in its *illustrated* phase runs remarkably close to our own; and Melbourne and Sydney can show papers which come very near to, if they do not quite equal, such journals as the *Graphic* and *Illustrated London News.*

It is unfortunate, in some respects, that in England a number of very cheap illustrated papers should have sprung up of recent years, which can hardly fail to exercise a malign influence on the young and ignorant, who are their principal supporters. I will not name names but one example of the evil is specially remarkable for its miserable daubs, and its extremely forced endeavours to make wit of a vulgar and offensive kind visible through the medium of a coarse and free pencil. It would, indeed, appear as though, in some quarters, it were the serious aim of men who, presumedly, should know better to vulgarise still more the vulgar and to vitiate the vicious, and that to a practically unlimited extent.

Fortunately, we have a strong counteracting influence in the many cheap forms of pure illustrated literature which should, and no doubt does, prove a great corrective to the evil referred to.

*Pari passu* with the development of cheap illustrated literature we have the evolution of an extraordinary amount of absolute moral literature copiously illustrated, which has for its publisher the Bill Sticker, and for its aims the advertising of something which is, or should be, in demand. Many of the pictures that are now seen on walls and hoardings are harmless enough, and may, and probably do, in no small degree, minister to the embryonic æsthetic culture of the multitude, but, *per contra*, many are of a decidedly opposite tendency, and it is a great pity that no kind of censorship can be enforced in regard to the preservation of the public roads and streets from what is vicious, brutalizing, or degrading, in the way of flaming posters, whether colored or plain.

# XI.—TRADE JOURNALS.

*Their Great Utility—Their Staple Contents—How they are
Managed—Advertisements—Advertisement Notices or Trade
"Puffs"—Meanness of some Firms—An Anecdote—The
Increasing Need for the Trade Journal—Class Literature
—The Ideal Newspaper—Mr. Goschen on Reading and
Thinking.*

PUTTING aside religious publications—to which one is
bound to assign the highest place—although few of
them carry out their ostensible mission—Trade Journals are
probably the most useful and harmless of all press organs.

Their number is rapidly increasing—naturally so with
the development of commerce, and a few of the number
are probably as near perfection in their respective lines, as
anything in the way of human endeavour can be.

Market Reports, Trade Statistics, and articles on
Finance and the movements of various Produce Markets
all over the world, make up the staple of their contents.

That one cannot, without going into purely technical
details, say very much about them, is a pretty good
evidence of their solidity and worth.

The story of the typical good man can be told in general in very few sentences, but the career of the knave requires a volume.

A Trade Journal avowedly depends for existence on advertisements, and many of these are obtained by the agency of literary notices.

The Publisher, who is always a smart go-ahead man—none other being of any use—uses all imaginable means to induce leading firms to have the specialities " puffed," and then suggests an advertisement as the well understood price of the " puff."

This is, indeed, legitimate enough, and it is the very basis of Trade Journalism which could not well exist if it were supported by circulation only, some really excellent and valuable Trade Papers having but very small *bona fide* subscription lists, and others again hardly anything at all in the way of a genuine sale.

Some firms have the meanness to manœuvre for "puffs" and then decline to give any equivalent.

They sometimes meet with their match.

In one instance of this kind the industrial reporter having taken unusual pains to prepare a long and an elaborate article, waited with the proof on the firm and after the literary points were satisfactorily adjusted, suggested the usual advertisement.

The firm objected and retorted that they had been asked to give the requisite facilities by the Reporter, and had done so, and were not obliged to do anything beyond.

" That is so," replied the Reporter, " I certainly did arrange this on the basis mentioned, but I happen to be Editor as well, and in that capacity I shall feel it a duty to my proprietors to cancel what I have done as Reporter, unless you give a fair equivalent."

The firm felt the force of this reasoning, and gave the required advertisement.

The present increasing development of Trade and the disquieting dependency of Great Britain on imports, is rapidly enhancing the value and importance of commercial Literature in all forms, and undoubtedly Trade Journalism will be enormously expanded in a few more years.

Every department in trade, must, sooner or later, have its special press exponent, and we may look to something phenomenal before long in this direction.

It has long been a serious consideration with the more thoughtful class of literary students as to what could be done eventually to effectually grapple with the flood of new books—some of which are undoubtedly necessary to read for purposes of culture, but such considerations are trivial compared with the problem presented by the Journals of the Future in Class, Trade, and Professional Literature.

These are increasing by scores, and are already far beyond the capacity of any individual to grasp.

The rate at which the Periodical Press grows may best be inferred from the following statistics, extracted from the *Newspaper Press Directory* for the year 1886. We learn thence that there were then published in the United Kingdom 2093 newspapers, distributed as follows :—England—London 409, provinces 1225—1634 ; Wales, 83 ; Scotland, 193 ; Ireland, 162 ; Isles, 21. Of these there were—144 daily papers published in England, 6 in Wales 21 in Scotland, 15 in Ireland, and 1 in the British Isles. In 1846 there were published in the United Kingdom 551 journals ; of these 14 were issued daily—*viz.*, 12 in England and 2 in Ireland ; but in 1886 there were established and circulated 2093 papers, of which no less than 187 were issued daily, showing that the Press of the country has nearly quadrupled during 40 years. The increase in daily papers has been still more remarkable; the daily issues standing 187 against only 14 in 1846. The magazines in course of publication, in 1886, including the Quarterly Reviews, number 1368, of which 397 were of a decidedly religious character, representing the Church of England, Wesleyans, Methodists, Baptists, Independents, Roman Catholics, and various other Christian communities.

Eventually, there will be a fine opening for a Journal whose sole object shall be to organise an exhaustive review of *every* department of Serial Literature, general, political, social, literary, scientific, religious, secular, critical, and in a word, to present periodically to its readers a summary of all that is really important and of general value in the current month.

The thought even of this almost turns one's brain, but what is it when compared to the gross outcome of even the contemporary Press?

Something like twenty five thousand well-written, fairly original articles probably issue every week from the British Periodical Press, and the number is increasing.

Literature of the book type is, being regularly and systematically run down into the shallow channels of the Serial Press and the whole nation is seriously threatened with what may be called intellectual water on the brain.

Is there no remedy for this?

Shall we eventually be divided into a number of cliques none of which, except in rare cases, will, or, indeed, can read each other's Literature?

Something very like this is already the case, and it is needless to say how seriously our culture as a people is being affected by the appalling substitute of quantity for quality in much of our current Literature.

That I am by no means alone in my views as to the great evils resulting from the haste and hurry, and the too generally superficial culture of the times is surely evidenced by many strong confirmations that have reached me quite recently. Thus, on February 27, 1886, Mr. Goschen, who, it is presumed, may be held as of some account on such a subject as the intellectual progress of the age, addressed at the Mansion House, London, a large gathering of students, of both sexes, members of the "London Society for the Extension of University Training," and delivered to them a rather noteworthy lecture on "Reading and Thinking." Dealing with the very same subject treated in the First Part of this work, Mr. Goschen, in regard to the two pressing and complex questions of the day—How and what to read, observed :—

"There was no doubt that one of the great drawbacks of readers of the present day was the mass of books produced, a matter which he regarded as one of the greatest dangers of our time, when coupled with the idea that one must read everything. People ordered from the library a book which had been recommended to them without asking themselves how it would fit into a course of systematic reading, and they got it and read it after a fashion. He would earnestly impress on them that it was not necessary to read everything which came out—that systematic reading would give more enjoyment and secure more profit. Instead of taking every dish, as at a German *talle d'hôte*, they should read *à la carte* in such quantities and qualities as they needed. The multiplicity of books, joined to the belief that all should be read, had led to the phenomena of the thirty pages of criticism and analysis of books in the old 'Quarterlies' being condensed into the fifteen pages of the modern magazines, and they in turn being further condensed in the daily papers. That process had a deleterious effect on serious reading in many ways, since mere dipping into so many subjects destroyed the capacity for serious work, which, though it might not give so much contemporary information, would do more to lift them out of their daily lives, by giving them access to the high and ennobling thoughts of the first authors of all countries. The mass of current literature was driving out the great classics of the present and the past; and he warned them against the tendency to waste time on such productions that should be devoted to serious work requiring thought. Wanting to read so much, led to hurried reading, which had become so much the fashion that even young ladies galloped through novels when they had plenty of time to read leisurely. With hurried reading there could be no studied reading. Such readers did not see the beauties of literature; and, not appreciating them, those beauties were no longer being created, beautiful writing becoming every day more and more rare. It was a well-recognised principle in dietetics not to bolt your food; neither should they bolt their mental food. A wholesome appetite should be supplied with wholesome mental food, which should be taken leisurely, that being the way in which the student would best thrive. They should not commit the fault sometimes committed in taking physical food, of picking too daintily and leaving half uneaten. That practice did not indicate a healthy appetite either in regard to food or to literature."

It need hardly be pointed out to the thoughtful reader that these utterances fully confirm very much advanced in this book, and coming to what is even more important than reading—*viz.,* thinking—the lecturer remarked :—

"Some people disagreed with everything they read—which, at any rate, indicated thought. A larger number agreed with everything they read, and, if they were really thinking, he had not much to say against the process; but the largest class of all consisted of those who read without thinking at all. Coming to what he would call original spontaneous thought, he was sorry to say that one of the greatest faults of the age was that thinking was going out of fashion, and that people thought less and less. That was partly due to the hurry of life, and partly due to mental indolence. Men were ready enough for negative criticism because the materials were before them to work upon; but they objected to the labour of finding their own materials. One of the most difficult forms of thought was to form the plan of an essay or a speech—to make a backbone; and rather than take the trouble to think out the problem and choose a line, men drifted, and got others to furnish them with suggestive remarks, instead of forming original spontaneous thought for themselves. Men thus got out of the habit of steady thought, and sank deeper and deeper into mental indolence."

# XII.—ADVERTISEMENTS.

*Advertisements—Their Interest—The World of " Wants "—*
*Candour of Advertisers—Baits and Traps for the Unwary—*
*Abuse of Advertising Columns.*

TO many persons, not the least interesting section of
the daily paper, is that devoted to advertisements.
The announcements, more especially in one or two of the
more popular organs of public opinion, furnish a very
accurate index to the social condition of the times, and are
in general much more to be relied on than the editorial
declarations as to the state of the country at large.

It is a wonderful sheet this, with, perhaps, 10,000
" Wants " of the most miscellaneous kinds. We see
before us the world as it is and each individual advertiser
proclaims through the medium of his modicum of space
his wants in a manner literally impracticable in many
cases under any other condition of things. Here in this
extraordinary vicarious market, crowds of people are free
to proclaim their miseries, their meanness, their greed,
their worst qualities in some cases, undeterred by even a
touch of shame. People seem to fancy, or at all events
some do, that print can cover any kind of moral abomination if it is merely an advertisement, and under the con-
cealment of initials, or some pseudonym, persons are found

daily advertising the utmost vileness of which human nature can well be guilty.

In the Daily Papers, to take a mild example, nearly all the Employment advertisements requiring large sums as *cash* security, are absolutely swindles. Many a contemtible scoundrel, who has not the stamina to stop even a tailor on the Queen's highway, takes to the pen instead of the pistol and with a drop of ink spreads his snare for the unwary throughout the length and breadth of the land.

A volume, nay, a library might be filled with examples. The common type is the bait of a clerkship advertised, in which the glib rascal who lays the trap, cunningly observes that previous experience is unnecessary, that the duties are light, the hours easy, the salary £2 10s. a week. The trifling condition is annexed that the successful candidate must deposit a cash security of £150 or £200!

Such advertisements appear daily, and numbers of simple people are duped and ruined through their agency. The Newspapers accepting such announcements, know their characters well, but profess to be unable to discriminate in such matters, and so the evil remains, and a gang of brigands are allowed to employ the matchless facility given them by the Daily Press for entrapping the unwary.

It is much the same, too, with other classes of objectionable advertisements. Liberty or rather License is pleaded as the reason why you must take the word of any unscrupulous quack that the medicine he advertises is as described, and, although in a word, some of the worst of criminals, male and female, are known to use the advertising columns for nefarious purposes, few Journals, indeed, ever deem it a duty to exclude whatever is calculated to defraud, mislead, or in any other way injure other people.

The *Times* is one of the few Journals that has resolutely and persistently set its face against this kind of thing, which is, unhappily, on the increase. In other words, the rogues who can use the pen and raise a little cash as an investment in the Devil's Funds, can reckon on commanding a stupendous circulation of the Daily Press of these islands.

Advertisements naturally lead to literary notices, and here again the Public often is grossly deceived and often outrageously victimised. Take the case of Public Companies' announcements. Well, the papers that get the advertisements as a rule, praise, and the papers that don't get the advertisement, abuse the projects. The Prospectus is usually stamped with the name of the Advertising agents, whence the advertisement has been sent, and this to the experienced eye of the Editor or Sub-Editor, says plainly as the English language can express it, " Please give a puff." In most cases this is done merely as an ordinary matter of business, without any intention of course of doing anybody harm. The men behind the scenes joke over such notices if they speak of them at all, which is not generally done and the transaction is regarded as a mere matter of routine.

Sometimes these Prospectuses come endorsed for " A good notice " and the Journalist is on his mettle. Does he investigate the project and ascertain whether it is really one which he would like to put his money into or that of his aged father or widowed mother? Oh ! dear no ! How could he ? He has the printed statement of the promoters and perhaps half an hour to do the eulogistic editorial in. Before he has time to reflect, and few Journalists ever do that while working, he has probably run off his cut and dried conventional introduction kept expressly for such occasions, and is prepared to inform a hundred thousand readers or perhaps a million that "amid the remarkable dearth of really safe and lucrative investments for the great class of small capitalists, &c., we have rarely met with an undertaking of so solid and promising a character as the project of which the prospectus now lies before us." Then he quotes the best bits that have been put in, very likely with the express purpose of deluding investors and the thing is done.

Newspapers above all things must pay, and the only problem that a conventional Editor ever takes any pains to solve, is how to procure with the greatest ease and the least cost, the greatest possible amount of sensational effect.

There are of course noble and singular exceptions to all this.

The *Hour* newspaper was one, and it ruined everybody connected with it, and when at last it finally died, some of the existing Journals rejoiced.

An intruder was gone and a perilous experiment had failed.

An assault had been made on Mammon, Conventionality, and Self-Conscious Respectability, and the issue had been ignominious defeat, for the Journal which took pure unadulterated Truth for its polar star.

# XIII.—ON LITERARY REMUNERATION.

### *Rates of Pay—Examples.*

VERY much nonsense has been published of late years regarding the remuneration given for Literary work.

Misrepresentation is obviously mischievous, and it is right to say a word on this head of Literary Technics, although at first it may rather disappoint some who doubtless think that the man whose "copy" is "accepted" pretty regulary, must necessarily be on the high road to riches.

First, as to Journalism proper.

The succesful journalist who has been right through the literary mill, and can report a meeting *in extenso*—descriptively, or condensed to a given space,—who can describe a flower show, criticise a new play or an opera, write a "Leader," if necessary, in an hour, or a series of more or less smart satirical notes on the news of the days, or, in a word, do anything that can be wanted in the way of "copy," may, if perfectly steady, quite temperate, and never ill, earn, on an average, one sovereign a day throughout the year.

Occasionally such a model journalist will make a little more, but then he will sometimes realise less, and £300 will be very near the mark of his income.

Now, £300 a year is surely very well, and certainly

contrasts most favourably with the usual emolument of even the best average clerks ; but let it be borne well in mind that to attain to and maintain that rate of earnings over a period of years, imperatively demands an uncommon combination of good bodily, moral, and mental qualifications.

And above all, such a pecuniary consummation is simply impossible, except there be superadded such a thorough knowledge of literary technics as has at last become a second nature.

Of course some writers make a great deal more, and obviously the value of a name in periodical literature is virtually an unknown quantity.

Directly a writer has established a reputation he may, within reason, usually make his own terms, but, of course, we are considering here simply the ordinary more or less cut and dried work of the anonymous writer, and obviously this being work that *any* trained journalist can take up, the market price, so to speak, cannot be very high.

The two following advertisements have been taken haphazard :—

"Sub-Editor. — Thoroughly competent, well-educated Sub-Editor for a daily paper. Salary, £200 per annum. Unexceptionable references. Apply, Phiz, care of A. B. and Co., Fleet Street, E.C."

" Wanted. — Managing Editor-Reporter. Halfpenny bi-weekly. Agricultural district. First-class local notes, leaderettes, &c. ; thoroughly practical proof-reader. None other. Salary 30s. and advertisement percentage. State age, politics, married or single, and enclose testimonials. Apply, first instance, P. E., Farringdon Road, London."

It will at once be seen that there is a great contrast in point of emolument here, and yet there is no doubt at all but that a goodly number of candidates sought the thirty shillings weekly, and the unknown percentage.

In numerous instances the young journalist must content himself with a pound a week.

As lately as the beginning of 1885, a well-known veteran writer complained in the *Athenæum* of the low average scale of remuneration offered to ordinary journalists.

" Even editors," he said, and the statement is fully corroborated by the advertisements cited above, " were offered by newspaper proprietors only £80 a year, and sometimes had to accept that beggarly remuneration because, unlike bricklayers," he bitterly added, " they have no union behind, to support them in standing out for an adequate salary."

This is certainly a *vexata questio.* It is hard to see how a " union " could mend matters, but the very best practical advice that can be given to the young writer is that he should strive with might and main, to be " thorough " in every department he attempts, that he should take the work nearest to his pen and exchange it for better when opportunity comes, and, in point of fact, opportunity always *does* comes to the helpful and progressive worker.

In truth, if we look into details, it will generally appear that the more poorly paid editorships do not involve six day's a week work, and a clever man, keeping his eyes open, will usually supplement his earnings as a contributor in other quarters.

As to the amounts to be made by contributions to the periodical literature, they vary from a few pounds a year to a thousand.

Most magazines have a fixed per-page rate, ranging from as little as five shillings, or seven and sixpence, to a guinea, or even more.

Leaders written by outside men, *i.e.*, those not on the permanent staff, are paid at rates varying from half a guinea to three guineas.   An industrious and known writer can earn large amounts as a contributor, especially if he be known to the editors of many periodicals.

# XIV.—LEGAL HINTS.

## *Agreements—Scales of Remuneration.*

WITH regard to Press Engagements of all kinds, a word on their legal aspects is in season.

First of all, there should be *written* agreements in all instances, and by adopting the obvious precaution of putting all points in black and white, much future trouble and possible loss will be prevented. Apart, however, from written agreements, wherein any kind of stipulation may be made, there are sundry "customs of the profession" which should be known to all its members in *esse* or *posse*. Thus the principle holds goods, that unless otherwise expressed, an editor is always entitled to six months' notice, a sub-editor to three, and a reporter simply, to one month.

The important principle that an editor can claim six months', and a sub-editor three months' notice, was recognised by the Judge of the Liverpool Bankruptcy Court, in a case tried before him on January 4th, 1883. The case was a claim preferred by Mr. J. Rintoul Mitchell, formerly chief sub-editor and leader writer of the *Liverpool Daily Mail*, against the trustees of the estate of that journal, and in the evidence of the expert witnesses it was clearly shown that the custom of the profession was precisely as stated above.

It is highly necessary to be armed with a written agreement, as newspaper proprietors are not in all cases absolutely honest in dealing with their employés, especially in cases where their journals may be losing heavily, and this tempts one to interpolate the remark, "that it is strange, indeed, to know that quite a large number of publications do not 'pay,' but, on the contrary, are continual losses to their unfortunate proprietors."

It is always wise not to let a paper drop behind in the matter of payments, but the young writer, who probably has only one publication open at a time, will, of course, find this difficult.

As to simple contributions, most publications have a scale of remuneration per page or column, by which the writer is bound. It has been ruled, too, that an editor's letter of acceptance of a contribution binds his proprietor to pay for it at the scale of the publication, and it is needless to add that all *paid* contributions become the absolute property of the journals in which they appear, and can only lawfully be reproduced by " permission " of the proprietor or conductor of the publications for which they have been actually purchased.

The rates of remuneration for original matter in newspapers and periodicals varies so much that it is virtually impossible to give in this place more than some general idea of the amount that may be thus earned. The lowest rates of remuneration for original matter is five shillings a column, whilst many papers pay a guinea for an ordinary article, and double that amount for a special leader. Columns and pages vary so greatly in capacity, owing to difference in size and type, that the higher price of some is nearly approximated as to quantity of matter involved, by the lower price of others.

It will be found, however, that if we take the minimum rates of remuneration for original contributions they are all higher for the work to be done than the rates of pay for sub-editorial work, and the industrious worker who can fill his available time with contributory work alone, will realise a larger income than the average all-round journalist.

# XV.—LIBEL.

LIBEL and the law thereof, so far as that can be practically explained to the non-legal mind, are obviously of much personal interest and moment to the young writer; more particularly if he be engaged in journalism, and very especially if he be occupied in any kind of editorial duty.

We say the *young* writer, because it may be presumed that the veterans of the Press will have no need to gather from books information that is pretty sure to be theirs as a matter of more or less personal experience, either in themselves or their friends, for actions of all kinds for libel naturally tends to multiply in these days of universal publicity, of much reckless writing, and of a general "rush into print" on the slightest pretext.

It goes without saying that the law even now, as amended, is eminently unsatisfactory, but possibly some readers may not be aware that by the Roman Law any libel clearly affecting adversely the reputation of another, was a capital offence.

In English Law anything published concerning another person, obviously calculated to do him injury, to lower him in the esteem of his neigbours, *i.e.*, that of the world, or even to render him ridiculous, is technically a libel, and until recently, the manifestly absurd and unjust maxim was permitted legal currency and countenanced even, that the greater the truth, the greater the libel.

The dispersion, *i.e.*, the publication of libels, was, in 1545, constituted a felony in this country, and all historical students are familiar with the terrible punishment inflicted on William Prynne for simply writing *Histriomastrix*, a mere condemnation of stage plays, construed into a libel on the Queen (1633).

Generally, the law was very harsh on this subject, and when, in 1791, Fox's Libel Bill, enlarging the discretionary power of juries, was presented to the Lords, that Assembly threw it out.

The Bill, however, which was much needed, passed in the following year.

In 1819 blasphemous or seditious libels on a second offence were made transportable offences, and it was not until 1840 that the persons engaged in Parliamentary reporting were really fully protected in the execution of their legitimate functions.

Three years later the severity of the law, as far as newspapers were concerned, was greatly relaxed by Lord Campbell's Act, 6 and 7 Vict., c. 96, and in 1868, in a famous case, Wason v. Walter (*The Times*), a Parliamentary report and reasonable comments thereon, were very properly pronounced no libel.

The remedy for libel is twofold. An action may be brought to recover damages, or compensation, or a criminal prosecution may be preferred.

Formerly, the plea of justification was not permitted, but

now it is allowed, although if put forward and not substantiated, it is held as a great aggravation of the original offence.

Many cases will immediately occur to the reader in which justification has been successfully pleaded.

With regard to journalism, it may be at once said that libel technically is much more frequent than is commonly supposed.

There are numerous published libels, especially in the daily papers, for which good grounds of action would lie, but the aggrieved parties do not prosecute, and happily it is becoming increasingly difficult for any libelled person to obtain legal redress unless he can come into court with perfectly clean hands.

Let the young journalist, however, make up his mind that knowingly he will not libel anybody, and this right habit once engendered he may sleep in peace, without fear of " trouble " at the office on the morrow.

Let it be remembered that to *copy* libellous statements, even while quoting the publication whence they are taken, constitutes itself a serious libel, the law very rightly not permitting this vicarious method of propagating libel.

One example is worth many rules in such cases as these.

A certain London firm of shipowners had a Government contract to send emigrants to a certain Australian colony.

As a matter of fact, the provisions provided were not good, and a leading Australian journal published an article severely commenting thereon.

The sub-editor of a London newspaper giving news from Australia for English readers, copied this libellous matter quite innocently, and as a mere item of intelligence.

He had, however, perpetrated a libel, and only escaped

by making a full printed apology for what subsequently proved to be a really truthful statement.

Perhaps, had this case been tried, the shipowners might have been defeated, but it is not certain, as they could hardly have been proved to know personally of the bad provisions, and " moral " assumptions in such cases have no legal value.

The young journalist who gets mixed up in a case of this kind is afterwards regarded with more or less suspicion by newspaper proprietors, for although, under some circumstances, a few journals may actually court prosecution for libel, ordinary steady-going respectable newspapers and periodicals hold the libel as an object of the greatest dread.

Journals of limited capital, and struggling for existence, may easily be wrecked over law expenses in this way, and all for a blunder that is as silly as it is unlawful.

Thus, in the case of publishing a List of Bankrupts there is serious risk of making a mistake in putting a man or men, as such, by mistake.

I knew a case where two brothers traded separately under the same name, and were distinguished only by their initials, " J." and " I."

It happened that the latter failed, but in a certain Trade journal the sub-editor allowed " J." to figure as the bank-rupt, and that little error, there being no malice whatever in the matter, cost the journal a large sum of money in the form of damages, and, of course, brought no credit of any kind, as libels are sometimes believed to do.

A hint should suffice to the cautious.

Let it not be supposed for one moment, however, that I would in any sense advise any public writer to refrain from full and proper comment on any matter worthy of such, or of passing the very sharpest censure on whatever is morally wrong.

To do this truly and bravely is equally a function and a duty of the publicist, but—and here comes the important limitation—do this without any libel.

It is quite easy.

Every libel is a blunder, too.

There never was a libel penned but an ordinarily good writer could produce on the same lines matter much more scathing to the person referred to, *and* entirely destitute of any actionable words.

Employ polished irony, keen sarcasm, biting satire, if necessary, but do not vulgarise your English by actionable expressions, merely abusive words, or anything in the nature of verbal shouting and calling of names, which only indicates the weakness of the writer.

Of course critical acumen is needed to discriminate between libellous and non-libellous matter, but by attending to this matter, and occasionally taking legal opinion on special points, the public writer can soon make himself pretty " safe."

The golden rule is to be careful, to resolve that knowingly he will not pen or re-produce a libel, and that whenever any passage in any matter for which he is responsible seems libellous, that he will blot it out.

# XVI.—THE RELIGIOUS PRESS.

*The Religious Press as it is—The Principal Organs—The want of Definiteness of Aim in so-called Religious Journals—Absence of an Earnest Faith—The Strength of Infidelity.*

THE Religious Press, to which I have alluded elsewhere, claims, of course, a separate consideration, and, if it does not occupy—as it should—the pride of place in this work, it is simply because its actual performance falls so far short of its magnificent opportunities and its strong statistical position as to number of organs and readers, that I regretfully as purposely place it in the rear of contemporary Journalism of which, surely, it should be the van-guard.

The Religious Press, in one sense, is historically very old, indeed, and it is not too much to say that as soon as Journals ceased to be simple news-letters, the religious spirit was rather strongly manifested in many of them. We will grant that the informing spirit was what would now be denounced as narrow and antiquated, out of date old-world notions, but the belief of the conductors of the leading Journals of the day was steadfast in God and in His Providence, and, like the old Puritans in opposing Tyranny, they did not deem it necessary to abandon their ancestral faith and pose as infidels. The vast majority of

the fifty or sixty principal so-called Religious organs are
of the present century, and few, indeed, date anterior to
the accession of Queen Victoria. The following are the
principal Religious newspapers, in the strict acceptation of
the term: *The Baptist* (established 1873); *British Friend*
(Glasgow, 1843); *Catholic Times* (1860); *The Christian*
(1869); *Christian Echo* (Cardiff, 1878); *Christian Globe*
(1874); *Christian Life* (1876); *Christian News* and *Press*
(both Glasgow, established respectively 1846 and 1877);
*Christian Signal* (1878); *The Christian Union* and *Christian
World* (respectively 1875 and 1856); *Church and State*
(1878); *Church Bells* (1871); *Church of England Temperance
Chronicle* (1873); *Church Review* (1861); *Church Times*
(1863); *Church Union Gazette* (1870); *English Churchman*
(1843); *English Independent* (1867); *Fountain* (1876);
*Freeman* (1855); *Friend* (1843); *Guardian* (1846); *Hand
and Heart* (1876); *Inquirer* (1842); *Jewish Chronicle* and
*Jewish World* (respectively 1841 and 1873); *Literary
Churchman* (1854); *Liverpool Protestant Standard* (1872);
*Methodist* (1874); *Methodist Recorder* (1861); *Morning Light*
(1878); *National Church* (1872); *Nonconformist* (1841);
*Primitive Methodist* (1866); *Record* (1828); *Rock* (1868);
*Scottish Guardian* (1870); *South London Gazette* (1878);
*Tablet* (1840); *Universe* (1860); *Watchman* (1835); *Weekly
Register* (1849); and *Weekly Review* (1862). These may be
taken as the main exponents of Religion in the United
Kingdom, and the first thing that strikes one in attempting
an analysis thereof, is that they are for the greater part
distinctly sectarian, and only Christian in the right and en-
lightened sense of the misused word, provided it happens
to be compatible with their particular mission, which is
usually some "ism," and a fierce crusade against some

objects which bear about the same relation to the real enemies that the Christian is called upon in this life to encounter and vanquish, that the windmill charged by Don Quixote did to the real antagonists he imagined them to be. The want of unity of purpose and common aim, is obvious when we consider that the sundry heads under which these newspapers appear, to follow an alphabetical order, are: Anglo-Catholic, Anti-Ritualistic, Baptist, Bible, Calvinistic, all forms of Militant Dissent, and general sectarianism. There are many, indeed, whose circulation and influence are very limited, but of some, like the *Christian World*, whose circulation is known to be very large, indeed, it is remarkable that the propagation of Christianity, pure and simple, ever seems subordinated to some kind of worldly motive such as Liberalism, for example, and thus the banner of the cross is too often degraded to be the mere insignia of a Party. By their own utterances we can judge these organs but too well. The leading articles that appeared during the great Gladstone Midlothian campaign, showed plainly that the " drum ecclesiastic " could be beaten to excellent Party purpose and that the things of this world, the sweets of office, the wielding of patronage, the pomp and circumstance of political triumph, were really more present in the Editorial mind than the true, solid, and enduring interests of that Christendom which has, alas! in these days such a woeful lack of real Champions who have the courage of their opinions, and who will not bargain with any of the myriad forms of the World, the Flesh, and the Devil, which are rampant in these latter nineteenth century days.

I do not write in a spirit of bitterness, nor of carping criticism. It might, surely, be well supposed that with all the splendid material advantages of contemporary culture, research, and progress generally, the Religious Press would, in this country—allowing, of course, some obvious exceptions—be the Christian Press, and that, if the Pulpits as a whole, lost power and influence, the writers for the avowedly religious journals would amply atone for the decay of true intellectual vitality in the Church. Is it so? As a broad rule, what are the so-called Religious Journals like from a literary view-point, and how much regard does the Positivist, the Agnostic, and the Atheist pay to these, the watch-dogs of the Christian fold? Possibly, when advancing the rant of the Salvationists, or delivering themselves of perfervid diatribes on the threadbare subject of Intemperance, there is a little earnestness and some spark of enthusiasm in the so-called Religious sheets, and so, too, may this be found when opportunity offers for expediting the evil day of National Secularism by advocating the Disestablishment of the Church. As to the editing and sub-editing of the majority of these Journals, it is too frequently simply contemptible from a professional view-point and, in general, when these organs attempt to " pronounce " on any purely religious point, the outside secular world pays not the least attention and, in truth, what they utter is, as one of Dickens's familiar creations would say, " of no consequence." Now, I don't desire to dogmatise ; I am fully aware how great a sacrifice is demanded, in these days, to the Fetish of Toleration, but I say that, while the ordinary thinker, writer, and speaker may feel it right to keep his own counsel in many grave matters, there is, for the avowedly Religious Press, but one just course open, when the fundamental principles of Christianity are seriously impugned and when its most sacred rites and its deepest mysteries, are profaned and made the subject of ineffable blasphemy. Then, indeed, should the brave word be spoken, and the banner of " no surrender " be displayed; then, indeed, the hour comes when a choice must be made, and when it becomes morally impossible to serve God and the World. But, what do we find? Search the files of these Journals during times of trial and mark the normal cautiousness, the trimming, the make-the-best-of-both-worlds spirit that commonly pervades these self-dubbed Christian writers. Now, mark, I do not say that Christian laymen generally are called on to denounce *secular* marriages. They can condemn them sufficiently by their conduct, and by the private expression of opinion, but the Religious Press ought not to countenance such a serious blow as is struck by the Registrar at true Christianity every time he officiates, when the Priest alone should make the marriage bond indissoluble, In like manner, no avowedly Christian Paper can consistently acquiesce, by the implied consent of silence, in the continued secularisation of National Education. The conductors of the Religious Press are Apostles of the Saviour or nothing, and they should vindicate, on all occasions and against all comers, the cardinal principles of a Christianity which will have none of any accursed thing, and will not strike any form of bargain with the spirit of Unbelief that is spreading so far and so fast throughout the length and breadth of the land. What do we need in our great Religious Journals?—simply men who would regard their respective organs as means for bringing about the consolidation of a Universal Christendom, a Christendom built solely on the lines of the Sermon on the Mount, and knowing no schism among Christians, but, at the same time, giving no quarter to unbelievers while persisting in infidelity. The Church Militant is no more, and it assuredly does not exist in its Press; but Atheism Militant marshals day by day the democratic forces to its cause and, day by day, the vantage ground, the strong entrenchments of the Christian, are stormed, and truly this storming is an easy task, for the Agnostic, the Positivist, the Atheist, has but to cry out "admit me into this stronghold of the faith—make me a teacher of Christian children—abolish these texts, and that oath—take away those hateful Christian symbols, they offend me—entrust to ME the making of the nation's laws"—and, then, when you—blind, weak, foolish, unfaithful and timid servants of the Master you betray—have won for us the victory, we will turn and rend you and show, that whatever may be the intolerance of the Christian bigot it is, at least, equalled by the Atheist who has once gained the prize of supreme earthly power.

This will, no doubt, sound extreme to many readers, but it may be noted that in one of the most incendiary speeches made, previously to the disgraceful scene of pillage that followed the Trafalgar Square Demonstration of the Unemployed, the necessity was insisted on for *Secular* Education. Do not imagine, luke-warm Christians, that in yielding to the Infidel, you will eventually be left in peace ; and, in truth, the stern lessons of history show that certain retribution, even in this life, invariably overtakes those who surrender up to evil the holy things and places they should defend with their lives.

In sober truth, if the Religious Press were animated by an ardent spirit like that which inspired a Jeremy Taylor, a Pascal, a Bossuet, or even a Paley, we should find a very different attitude presented towards it by the outside world. If the Religious Press were in earnest—like the early missionaries to the Orient from the Catholic countries of the West, we should see many a victory gained over the world itself, and many a splendid triumph of Christian thought and principle.

I have borne, as it may appear, rather heavily on the Religious Press, but when we survey the existing situation from a purely Christian view-point, we must admit that we live in evil days. Once, indeed, too, the Press occupied the more subordinate place in the great Republic of Letters, and it mattered little what it did or said. Now, however, it is entirely different, and if it be of much national moment as to what is the attitude of the avowedly Secular Press towards Religion, much more is it of moment as to what is the spirit and tone of the so-called Christian Papers which are avowedly put forth to promote, by every lawful means, the advancement of the Christian Religion and the defeat and utter subjection of every form of Infidelity and Unbelief. Everywhere around us blow after blow is being dealt at the very bases of all forms of Revealed Religion and—probed to the bottom, that is—apart from any kind of mere dogma, the sole guarantee for the maintenance, in its integrity, of FAMILY LIFE as we understood it, and for the continued preservation of morality.

# APPENDIX.

THE subject of Copyright in its current legal aspects has been generally dealt with in the First Part of this book, but a few remarks on some obvious features of this great and important subject, seem required on some points not touched in Part I. and, also, because since that was in type the Government Bill to amend the Law respecting International and Colonial Copyright, has been issued. Briefly, this measure has for its object to empower the Queen to carry into effect, at home and in the colonies, the Convention agreed to at the International Conference at Berne, in September, 1885. By the existing Acts an order in Council may direct that as regards literary and artistic works first issued in a foreign country, the author shall have copyright not exceeding the period for which home authors of like works have copyright. Now, the Berne Convention gives authors of literary and artistic works, published in any country which is a party to the Convention, copyright in all other countries which were parties to it. By the Government Bill referred to, the laws of English Copyright are brought into full harmony with this arrangement. It is distinctly laid down that in certain cases the publisher in the United Kingdom of the work of a foreign author may take proceedings, as though he were owner of the copyright. In cases of simultaneous production, an Order in Council may settle for purposes of copyright in which country the work was first produced; and, if it is a foreign country, the copyright will be such as exists by virtue of its production in that country, and not the copyright of the United Kingdom. Foreign authors are to have for ten years, or such other term as the Order in Council prescribes, the right to prevent the production or importation into the United Kingdom of a translation. The Bill applies to existing works, and with the reservation of power by Order in Council to exclude any of the colonies, it applies the provisions of the International Copyright Acts to the colonies. This appears progress in a right direction, but is it enough, and have we, as a nation, yet attained to a really clear notion of what is equitable in regard to the rights of Literary property and very especially the rights of the author thereof?

It has been said that the idea of a right of property in literary composition is of modern origin, and we know that lawyers have seriously asked, in days of old, how could ideas, or the manner of writing a narrative, be converted into property, or, it was said, if this can be so, it would be reasonable to conclude that the property should be made absolute and perpetual to the owner and his heirs. These and similar questions are said to have greatly exercised the minds of English jurists of the eighteenth century. In reality—at least, to my own view of the matter—all property may be open to question as to whether it really vests in the community or in the individual, but this form of Socialism which, being rightly interpreted, means spoliation and downright plunder, in the name of a community of robbers—need not be further considered here, and it must be obvious, as a matter of common sense, that if property can exist in anything, it can do so in literary composition, as much as in any other form of human creative energy. The strictly metaphysical, *i.e.*, the intangible and, to us, the Invisible, must necessarily form the true base of all *things*, to use the popular word, of which we have tactical or visual knowledge, idea, or conception, being, in point of fact, the original of all human productions. Surely it was in following out this train of reasoning that Dr. Johnson, dealing with literary property, observed :—

" There seems to be in authors a stronger right of property than that by right of occupancy : a metaphysical right, a right as it were of creation which should, from its nature, be perpetual."

It is true that Dr. Johnson admitted that to allow perpetuity to the rights of an author to his work, might be against public policy as, he remarks, no book could be annotated, should the author persistently object, and then the Doctor, not always equally luminous in his views, states that valuable books once created by an author and issued, should be understood as belonging to the world. This last is, probed thoroughly, a pure and illogical assumption and simply an after-thought, prompted by ideas of the community being more than the individual, and, remembering himself immediately, a natural instinct of justice induced that good and great man to add that " the author is entitled to an adequate reward." Truly, this is so—but how often does he obtain it? The evil is that originally authors were obliged to find their pecuniary reward in the bounty of *individual* patrons of Literature and by the time the Publisher came to be substituted for the Patron, it unfortunately happened that all notion of a distinct individualised PROPERTY in the offspring of a man's brain had been lost, for it is absurd to suppose that when seriously examined by the light of Equity, much, if any, doubt could really exist as to the question, and writers like Plato or Aristotle, would, no doubt, have stoutly insisted that their original thoughts were their property and could not, logically, be appropriated by others. Copyright, however, has not inaptly been called the youngest child of Civilization, and now that the national mind has been thoroughly awakened to the whole of the subject, we may hope for some equitable finality therein. It has been remarked that there is this difference between copyright and other kinds of property—that wherever copyright has been recognised as property, it has been especially protected by statute, and limited for varying terms of years. In France copyright lasts for the author's life and, subject to sundry regulations, for half a century more. In Germany it is the same, only the after-death period is limited to thirty years. In Austria it is as in Germany. In Holland copyright lasts for life, and twenty years after ; in Denmark for life and thirty years after ; in Sweden for life and twenty years ; in Russia for life and twenty-five years ; and ten years more if an edition is published within five years of the close of the first term. In Greece, strangely enough, copyright runs only for fifteen years from publication ; but in Italy for life and forty years after, with a second term of like duration during which, however, anybody may publish the work by paying a Royalty to the author ; and, in Belgium copyright lasts for life and twenty years after. In the United States copyright is limited to twenty-eight years, and fourteen years more if the author, or certain of his representatives, be living and the title be recorded anew six months prior to the expiration of the first period of twenty-eight years. Surely this—varying as are the details—demonstrates absolutely that, by a consensus of opinion mankind recognises the fact that there *is* an individual property in a literary work and, if we view the whole subject carefully, it will certainly appear that Literature—Authors and Publishers —would all be enormous gainers, if only literary works could be once permanently put on the same intelligible basis as any other kind of property, so that those dealing therein would know what was before them, as fully as though they were dealing in furniture, houses, or land, and thus the utmost encouragement would be given, from a commercial view-point, to all engaged either in the production or diffusion of Literature. This is, perhaps, a view not as yet generally taken of the complex Copyright problem but, surely, it is one equally in harmony with common sense and justice, and, as it would greatly stimulate all workers in the vast and increasing literary fields of the present, it is obvious that the public would benefit too, and thus it would be found at last by allowing *full* individual rights of property in literary productions, the community would actually gain, and what was wrongly supposed, by a former age, to be *against* public policy, would actually prove to be altogether in its favor.

## FINIS.

London—Printed by the London Literary Society, 376, Strand, W.C.

SUPPLEMENTARY

# LIST OF PUBLICATIONS

ISSUED BY THE

# LONDON LITERARY SOCIETY,

## 376, STRAND, LONDON, W.C.

# NOVELS.

## Zig-Zag,

"A Study of Society." By GERTRUDE M. IRELAND BLACKBURNE, (Author of "Algernon Sydney," a Review, 1 vol.). 470 pp., crown 8vo., cloth, 6/-.

" *Zig-Zag* is a clever book, with much more in it than is found in most novels in our day of high-pressure writing. The characters are well drawn, the plot consistently worked out."—*Morning Post.*

"Her book is worthy of the very highest praise. . . . It is full of a movement and an intense feeling which leave a lasting effect on the mind of a reader."—*Whitehall Review.*

" *Zig-Zag* is a clever book."—*Academy.*

"We can safely speak of *Zig-Zag* as being a clever story, showing much liveliness and good taste. The interest does not flag."—*Publishers' Circular.*

"A very straightforward story."—*Fun.*

"The work is undoubtedly clever."—*Court Journal.*

"A really noteworthy book."—*Chester Chronicle.*

## Two Loves in One Life.

(2 vols.), crown 8vo., 21/-.

"These two volumes of domestic fiction form a really good story. . . . The characters are each and all well-drawn, natural and life-like. . . . The tale is well constructed and interesting."—*Morning Post.*

"Of the order of pretty stories; the women's characters are best. Lady Elizabeth is particularly well done."—*Saturday Review.*

"The best book we have read for some time."—*Sunday Times.*

"Reader's attention engaged throughout."—*Queen.*

"This is a good story, and the writer, whenever the name is disclosed, will have achieved a reputation."—*Bookseller.*

"The style is very pure."—*Whitehall Review.*

"The story-teller concentrates all his interest on the tale, and manages to inspire his readers with a contagious interest."—*Literary World.*

"Striking situations."—*Spectator.*

"This book possesses many passages of great power, many touches of true tenderness, and considerable skill in construction and characterism."—*Fun.*

"The characters are singularly original, the story exciting without too much sentiment or sensation, and the work is, in fact, a novel of our times."—*Birmingham Daily Post.*

"Written in a simple natural manner. The last few chapters in the book contain much that is decidedly pathetic."—*Court Journal.*

"The incident is a striking one, and very different from those usually met with in novels."—*Academy.*

## Judged by Appearances.

By ELEANOR LLOYD, (Author of "Valeria, A Tale of Venice," 1 vol.; and "The Langdales of Langdale End," 1 vol.). 343 pp., crown 8vo., cloth, 6/-.

"The characters are clearly defined, and the incidents well described."—*Morning Post.*

"A very enjoyable book."—*Lady's Pictorial.*

"Tales of the Civil Wars are seldom void of interest, and Miss E. Lloyd's story is no exception to the rule. Various well-drawn word-pictures of the period, a sufficiently interesting plot, and a number of interesting characters make the volume very readable."—*Society*.

"Is told with an animation, piquancy, and 'go' that will make it a popular bit of romance."—*Freeman's Journal*.

"The incidents are well told."—*Guardian*.

"A well written and thoughtful book."—*Literary World*.

"The tale abounds with interest."—*People*.

## A Heroine of the Commonplace.

By M. DAL VERO, (Author of "Francis: A Socialistic Romance," 1 vol.). 370 pp., crown 8vo., cloth, 6/-.

"The character of the heroine is singularly sweet and unassuming."—*Morning Post*.

"Thoroughly recommended as a gift book of unusual excellence. It is a high toned story, picturing the nobleness and beauty of self-sacrifice with a quiet force and simple reality which will continually remind the reader of Miss Yonge. The plot is ingeniously managed, with incident and interest enough to carry readers of any age through all the story, without desiring to miss a single page, till they arrive at a most unexpected and somewhat sensational conclusion in the closing chapter."—*Guardian*.

"Dal Vero has the gift, and no mean one it is, of letting her readers *see* the scenes and people she describes—not merely read about them."—*Literary World*.

"The *dénouement* is decidedly uncommonplace, and is both natural and original."—*Lady's Pictorial*.

"A wholesome and interesting story. . . . The book as a whole is readable and pleasant."—*Society*.

"There is a vast amount of good material in this book."—*Bookseller*.

"A pleasant and wholesome story."—*Scotsman*.

"Readable with real pleasure."—*Court Circular*.

## Arlegh Clough.

By HAMO DOKENFELD. 304 pp., crown 8vo., cloth, 3/6.

"The story is constructed soundly."—*Saturday Review*.

"The different scenes are painted with vividness and feeling."—*Spectator*.

"Is, without doubt, a clever story."—*Morning Post*.

"As good as the thousand novels produced during the year."—*Lady's Pictorial*.

"Altogether the tale is tragic and well told."—*Bookseller*.

## Played out and Lost.

By AMY HURLSTON, (Author of "Barbara Allen"). 262 pp., crown 8vo., cloth, 6/-.

"A clever study."—*Literary World*.

"Very readable."—*Birmingham Gazette*.

"Will be devoured by sentimental young ladies."—*Morning Post*.

## Ferndyke.

A Realistic Novel. By CLAUD HARDING, R.N. 343 pp., crown 8vo., cloth, 6/-

"Interest never flags. . . . A well-constructed plot."—*Morning Post*.

## Ian Roy.

Sensational One Shilling Railway Novel (bound in boards), and with special design on cover. By URQUHART FORBES (Author of "Otterstone Hall," 2 vols.).

## Douglas Archdale.

A Tale of Lucknow. By C. M. KATHERINE PHIPPS, (Author of "The Sword of de Bardwell," 1 vol.; and "Who is the Victor?" 1 vol.). 230 pp., crown 8vo., cloth, 6/-.

"A very pleasant and interesting tale."—*Bristol Daily Post*.

"Told with considerable ability and certainly interesting."—*Sheffield Daily Independent.*

"The whole story is pure in motive, and the style is graceful."—*Cork Examiner.*

## Life's Changes.

By Mrs. WILMETT MARYON. 260 pp., crown 8vo. (bevelled boards), cloth, 2/6. (*2nd edition*).

"An interesting story, and well told. The different characters are ably delineated, and the tone of the book is excellent."—*Christian Age.*

"The stories are well interwoven with each other, and readers . . . cannot fail to be interested in the book."—*Christian World.*

"It is not often that a novel combines so many literary, dramatic, and moral excellences as this one."—*Oldham Chronicle.*

## Brought to Repentance.

By FREDERICK AUBREY. (New edition). 430 pp., crown 8vo., cloth, 6/-.

## Marion; or, the Mystery of Robesdale.

By R. SEBRIGHT SCHOLES, (Author of "Carswell Grange," 1 vol.). 286 pp., crown 8vo., cloth, 3/6.

"Excellent sketches of characters."—*Morning Post.*

"Possesses a good deal of descriptive power."—*Liverpool Mercury.*

"Is a romance of absorbing interest. The diction is concise and vigorous."—*Liverpool Daily Post.*

## The Heiress Against her Will.

By LILIAN DUDLEY FIELD. 245 pp., crown 8vo., cloth, 2/6.

## Her World.

250 pp., crown 8vo. (bevelled boards), cloth, 2/6.

"The story is interesting."—*Fun.*

## Sister Undine.

By ANNIE MONKTON LONG. 250 pp., crown 8vo. (bevelled boards), cloth, 2/6.

"Most pleasantly written tale."—*Sunday Times.*

"A well-written tale."—*Literary World.*

## The Chimes of Erfurt.

Translated from the German, by BEATRICE TOMASSON and CÄCILIE WÜSTENBURG. 215 pp., crown 8vo., cloth, 3/6.

"'Hans Sachs, the cobbler bard—laureate of the gentle craft,' as Longfellow calls him in his poem on Nuremberg, is a conspicuous character in this early Sixteenth Century Tale, which is quaintly interesting and artistically meritorious."—*Daily Telegraph.*

"A very pretty story, carefully and intelligently translated."—*Lady's Pictorial.*

"A lively sketch of real German life at Nuremberg."—*Graphic.*

"Thoroughly wholesome and interesting tale."—*Guardian.*

## The Story of a Moorish Knife.

By GERTRUDE R. HENDERSON. 177 pp., crown 8vo., cloth, 2/-.

## The Beautiful Lady Chichester.
By ANNA M. MONRO. 3/6.

## Through Cloud and Sunshine.
By E. L. SEVORG. 3/6.

## At Home Farm.
By EMILY CROXFORD. 2/6.

## Still Waters.
BY CRANSTONE BROOKS. 240 pp., crown 8vo., cloth, 3/6.

## Blessing or Curse.
By LOUISE A. VANE. 220 pp., crown 8vo., cloth, 2/6.

## Evening Shadows.
By EMILY DUNFORD. 200 pp., crown 8vo., cloth, 2/6.

# BOOKS FOR PRESENTATION.

## The Story of Jack Harding.
His Schooldays, College Life, His Crime. By WALTER HOWSON. 240 pp., crown 8vo., cloth, 3/6, (bevelled boards). (*2nd edition.*)

"Really good features."—*Athenæum.*
"Extremely readable and full of movement."—*Literary World.*
"Original and clever."—*Morning Post.*
"Mr. Walter Howson's *Jack Harding* is a cleverly-told and interesting story."—*Court Journal.*
"The author has conceived an entirely new way of amusing a jaded public."—*Whitehall Review.*
"The incidents are worked up in a vigorous way."—*Queen.*

## Old Tales and Legends for Young People.
By ANNETTE L. DAVEY. Illustrated by Edward O. Davey. (Full page illustrations). 60 pp., 4to, cloth, 2/6, (*2nd edition*).

"Told with point and spirit."—*The Times.*
"A charming collection of nursery stories. Illustrations greatly enhance the appearance of the Book."—*Pall Mall Gazette.*
"The illustrations are of considerable merit."—*Globe.*
"Fresh and entertaining volume. . . . Will have much interest for modern readers."—*Daily Chronicle.*
"Well told and cleverly illustrated. A rarely excellent volume."—*Society.*
"Well written, and admirably adapted for presentation."—*Morning Post.*
"Excellent production. We heartily commend it to all those who are anxious to provide their young friends with stories which will delight and amuse them."—*Sunday Times.*
"The stories from Scandinavian mythology are well written, and improve as they go on, the Legends of Roland are very pretty, and the illustrations accompanying them are good."—*Guardian.*

## Nænia: or Voices from the Silent Land.
(Allegories.) 220 pp., crown 8vo., cloth, 2/6. (*2nd edition*).

"This is a series of parables ingeniously written and founded on the growth of flowers and other phenomena of the garden. . . . The chapters are written in simple language and a lively style."—*Queen.*

"It is a pretty fancy which gives soul and speech to flowers. . . . This charming allegory, which seems to have been written principally for the young, is in many ways superior to the tales destined generally to amuse their leisure hours."—*Morning Post.*

"A thoughtful and well-written work. Readers who admire literary skill, but above all value religious teaching, will like it much. Quiet, simple, and of a tender tone, its pleasing fable lessons—the voices of birds and flowers—will win their way."—*Churchman.*

"Simple, easy, and graceful."—*Guardian.*

## Pixies and Nixies.

By EDITH MARY SHAW. 205 pp., crown 8vo., cloth, 3/6.

"Original and selected."—*Daily Telegraph.*

"Is a book in which the young folks will certainly find amusement."—*Spectator.*

"Very good entertainment."—*Queen.*

"A light, bright, pleasant volume, written in an attractive manner."—*Reynold's Weekly News.*

"The excellent tone, and the graceful verses which are scattered through its pages, should make it popular."—*Society.*

"A charming book, . . . is written with real genius."—*Guardian.*

## Two Phials and a Talisman.

By HANDOIS. 96 pp., crown 8vo., cloth, 2/6.

"A bright little fairy tale."—*Morning Post.*

"Children will follow the incidents with interest."—*Literary World.*

## The Music of a Merry Heart.

(A Biographical Sketch.) By EDWARD LE CLERC. 308 pp., crown 8vo., cloth, 6/0.

## The Secrets of Pinland.

(Profusely Illustrated.) By ANNA M.F. JOHNSON, (Author of "Haydon's Gully," and "Harptree Coombe"). 2/6.

## Drama for the Drawing Room.

By Mrs. L. DEBENHAM. 130 pp., crown 8vo., cloth, 3/0.

## Paris and the Parisians.

Edited by MAJOR-GENERAL NORGATE. 260 pp., crown 8vo., cloth, 2/6.

"It is to some extent worth knowing what Paris looked like in 1816 to a solid English clerical gentleman. We can, therefore, recommend 'Paris and the Parisians.'"—*Saturday Review.*

"A very interesting Diary."—*Daily Chronicle.*

"A faithful record of observations made during a visit to Paris in 1816."—*Army and Navy Gazette.*

## Lawn Tennis.

(Profusely Illustrated.) By R. H. ORPHEN. 1/0.

"A curious idea worked out with considerable skill."—*Army and Navy Gazette.*

"Exceedingly amusing."—*Bookseller.*

"Well illustrated and interesting."—*Weekly Times.*

"A close study of the popular game is evidenced in many of these sketches, which combine fidelity to nature with a spirit of genuine drollery."—*Daily Chronicle.*

"Cleverly drawn, and display considerable humour. Mr. Orpen's drawings will be a welcome addition to the literature of the tennis tea-table."—*Morning Post.*

## Cupid's Darts, or Remarkable Love Letters.

Including, amongst others, letters by the following celeb-
rities : The Earl of Peterborough, Henri IV., Byron,
Burns, Berlioz, Bolingbroke, Lord Nelson, Goethe, Lucien
Bonaparte, Petrach, Charles Dickens, Charles Mathews,
Lady Morgan, Martin Luther, James V. of Scotland,
Charles I. of England, Shelley, Kean, etc., etc. 266 pp.,
crown 8vo., cloth, 2/6 (bevelled boards).

" A charming collection of amatory epistles penned by famous men and
women."—*Daily Chronicle.*
" These letters contain a good deal that is curious and amusing."—*Queen.*
" A very readable series of letters."—*Yorkshire Post.*

# THEOLOGICAL.

## What is the Church?

Dealing with the study of The Old Testament, The New
Testament, The Church of Christ's Baptism, Sacrifice,
Holy Communion, The Church and the World, On Aposto-
lical Succession, Worship, The Church of England, The
position of the Sects. By A. COLLES, M.D. 309 pp.,
crown 8vo., cloth, 5/-, (*2nd edition*).

" A thoroughly sensible and common-sense guide to the devotional aspects
of religious rights and communion."—*Literary World.*
" It is a very excellent work . . . particularly well done . . .
written with much judgment and discretion. This work is admirably adapted
to its purpose. . . . We heartily commend its contents."—*Church Times.*
" An able work. . . . We repeat our high opinion of the ability of the
author, and we cordially recommend his book to all."—*Christian Globe.*

## Darius the Median Identified ; or, the True Chronology of the Ancient Monarchies Recovered.

Containing a Complete and Harmonious Arrangement of
the Chronologies of the Monarchies of Judah, Israel,
Egypt, Assyria, Babylon (or Chaldea), Lydia, Media, and
Persia. The Identifications of " Pul," " Asnapper," and
" Sardanapalus," Kings of Assyria ; " Darius the Median "
and " Belshazzar," Kings of Babylon ; " Cyrus," " Ahasuerus," and " Artaxerxes," Kings of Medo-Persia ; and
" Esther," Queen of " Ahasuerus." The Dates of the
Invasions of Judea by the Armies of Sennacherib, Holo-
fernes, and Nebuchadnezzar : of Asia by the Scythians
(with a Vindication of its Duration for 28 Years as affirmed
by Herodotus): of Egypt by Cambyses and Darius the
Persian ; and of the Fall of the Cities of Nineveh, Sardis,
and Babylon, etc., etc. Also, a Detailed Chronological
Adjustment of the Events of the " Return "—from the Fall
of Babylon to the Completion of the Building of the Wall
around Jerusalem by Nehemiah ; and Compendium of
Sacred and Secular Chronology from about B.C. 1000 to
about B.C. 200. By CHARLES FULKES WATSON. 250 pp.,
crown 8vo., cloth, 3/6.

"Mr. Watson writes very learnedly on a very abstruse subject."—*England.*

"Great industry and research must have worked to produce this book, which aims at settling once for all the personal identity of the great monarch of antiquity, and proving that Daniel is historically in harmony with the researches of eminent Assyriologists. The point is argued with much ability; and chronological tables are added as further evidence of the writer's judgment being correct."—*Bookseller.*

## A Theory of Creation.

By the Rev. J. C. WHISH, M.A. 250 pp., crown 8vo., cloth, 6/-.

"It is an earnest attempt to prove the truth of the Scriptural History."—*Ecclesiastical Gazette.*

## 1451 Questions and Answers in Church Services.

By the Rev. H. HUTCHINGS, M.A. 3/-.

## Sermons.

By the Rev. HARBART TANNER. 3/-.

# MISCELLANEOUS WORKS.

## Memories of India.

By Colonel JAMES CURRIE. 120 pp., crown 8vo., cloth, 2/6.

## Wealth Work and Want.

An examination of the existing social condition, its evils and proposed reform. By EDWIN ADAMS. 140 pp., crown 8vo., cloth, 1/-.

"A thoughtful and stimulating inquiry."—*Hereford Times.*
"Thoughtful and well written book."—*Western Morning News.*
"Commands considerable public attention."—*Sussex Daily News.*
"Of interest to those who are concerned with the social problems of the day."—*Queen.*
"An exceedingly and well written discussion."—*Western Daily Mercury.*
"Calm and able discussion. Well worth study."—*Birmingham Daily Post.*

## Reaction of Gravity in Motion; or the Third Motion of the Earth.

Treating upon the Mechanism of Motion, Kepler's Law of the Equal Distribution of Areas, the Newtonian Theory, etc. By TREVIGRA. 1/-.

"Altogether a very profound book on an obscure subject."—*Literary World.*
"Has created some considerable sensation in the scientific world, is worth reading, being evidently the work of long study."—*Society.*

## My Experiences as a Moderate Drinker, a Drunkard, and Total Abstainer.

With "A Rill from the Town Pump," By NATHANIEL HAWTHORNE. By CHARLES MEADOWS. 2/-.

"The book is certainly characterised by more liberal-mindedness than most works of the kind."—*Society.*

## POETICAL WORKS.

### Gordon, and other Poems.

By GEORGE ABEL. 300 pp., crown 8vo., cloth, 3/6.
"Admirable work."—*Sussex Daily News.*
"Mr. Abel has a clever and facile pen."—*Christian World.*
"Shows considerable talent."—*City Press.*
"Well worth presenting to the public."—*Broad Arrow.*

### Claudio and Fida, and other Poems.

By ASTON CLAIR. 127 pp., crown 8vo., cloth, 3/6.
"The titular piece is a tragic and pathetic story, told in good verse, easy and agreeable to read, and with a fervid energy, a sympathetic enthusiasm, which carries the reader unhalting to the end."—*Illustrated London News.*
"Highly commendable."—*Court Journal.*
"There is a softness and sweetness pervading the whole, which at once engages the sympathy of the poetic mind."—*Bookseller.*

### Volume of Poems.

By the Rev. P. SOUTHMEAD GLUBB, B.D. 3/6.

### Volume of Poems.

By HOWARD DEAZELEY, M.A. 3/6.

### Volume of Poems.

By the Rev. F. ELSON. 3/6.

### The Modern Titan.

A Drama. By R. D. SINCLAIR. 2/6.

### Poems for Recitation.

By BENSLEY THORNHILL. 1/-.

### Volume of Poems.

By Mrs. C. S. SHREWSBURY. 6/-.

### Volume of Poems.

By H. R. DECK. 1/-.

### Volume of Poems.

By CYGNET. 3/6.

## PAMPHLETS.

### Party Politics and the Social Question.

By ÆON. 6d.

### Practical Policy; or, Resume Gladstoniana.

By the Rev. W. CLOSE, M.A. 6d.
"We advise all Conservatives to secure this book."—*Norwich Argus.*
"Smartly written."—*People.*

### The Duty of the Clergy towards Politics.

By ONE OF THEMSELVES. 6d.

### Protestant Dissenters.

A Tract for the Times. 9d.

### The Marquis's Own.

By Lieut-Col. SILVER. 6d.